# SEALS, FINGER RINGS,
# ENGRAVED GEMS AND AMULETS IN THE
# ROYAL ALBERT MEMORIAL MUSEUM,
# EXETER

*For Lawrence*

# SEALS, FINGER RINGS, ENGRAVED GEMS AND AMULETS IN THE ROYAL ALBERT MEMORIAL MUSEUM, EXETER

from the Collections of

Lt. Colonel L.A.D. Montague and Dr N.L. Corkill

by

SHEILA HOEY MIDDLETON

Photographs by Robert Wilkins

Published by Exeter City Museums

1998

Published with grant aid from the
Heritage Lottery Fund and Devon County Council

**Heritage Lottery Fund**

ISBN: 1-85522-587-5

Produced for Exeter City Museums by Sutton Publishing Ltd,
Phoenix Mill, Thrupp, Stroud, Glos, GL5 2BU

Printed by Bookcraft, Midsomer Norton, Somerset

*Front cover illustration*: a ring set with a cornelian gem showing
the draped bust of a bearded god (no. **32**).

# Contents

ACKNOWLEDGEMENTS . . . . . . . . . . . . . . . . . . . . . . . . . . . . . . . . . . . . . . . . . . . . . . . . . vii

FRONTISPIECE . . . . . . . . . . . . . . . . . . . . . . . . . . . . . . . . . . . . . . . . . . . . . .(facing) viii

INTRODUCTION . . . . . . . . . . . . . . . . . . . . . . . . . . . . . . . . . . . . . . . . . . . . . . . . ix

NOTES ON THE CATALOGUE ENTRIES . . . . . . . . . . . . . . . . . . . . . . . . . . . . xix

**CATALOGUE**

I   ANCIENT NEAR EASTERN:                                                          I

Cylinder seals **1–26** (pre-3000 BC–7th century BC) . . . . . . . . . . . . . . . . . . . . . . . .   3

Stamp seals **27–9** (7th–ca.3rd century BC) . . . . . . . . . . . . . . . . . . . . . . . . . . . . . . .   28

II   GREEK and ROMAN:                                                             35

Rings, intagli and sealings:

Greek **30–1** (4th–ca.2nd century BC) . . . . . . . . . . . . . . . . . . . . . . . . . . . . . . . . . . . .   37

Greco-Roman **32–3** (1st century BC) . . . . . . . . . . . . . . . . . . . . . . . . . . . . . . . . . . . .   41

Roman Deities **34–42** (ca.1st century BC–ca.3rd century AD) . . . . . . . . . . . . . . . .   44

    Portraits **43–4** . . . . . . . . . . . . . . . . . . . . . . . . . . . . . . . . . . . . . . . . . . . . . .   54

    Animals, combinations, symbols etc. **45–51** . . . . . . . . . . . . . . . . . . . . . . . . .   56

    Magic gems **52–4** . . . . . . . . . . . . . . . . . . . . . . . . . . . . . . . . . . . . . . . . . . . .   64

    Devon finds **55–61** . . . . . . . . . . . . . . . . . . . . . . . . . . . . . . . . . . . . . . . . . . .   70

    Roman lead sealings **62–5** . . . . . . . . . . . . . . . . . . . . . . . . . . . . . . . . . . . . . .   78

III  SASSANIAN and BACTRIAN:                                                                                    83

Stamp seals, ringstones, ring **66–82** (ca.3rd century–7th century AD) . . . . . . . . . . . . .   84

Bactrian ringstone **83** (ca.2nd century AD or later) . . . . . . . . . . . . . . . . . . . . . . . . . .   101

IV  RENAISSANCE AND MODERN:                                                                                     103

Ringstones **84–6** (ca.16th–19th century AD) . . . . . . . . . . . . . . . . . . . . . . . . . . . . .   104

V  AMULETS AND MISCELLANEOUS:                                                                                   108

Amulets **87–97** (ca.2nd millennium BC–19th century AD?) . . . . . . . . . . . . . . . . . . .   109

Miscellaneous **98–103** (from antiquity to the 18th or 19th century AD) . . . . . . . . .   119

ABBREVIATIONS AND SELECT BIBLIOGRAPHY . . . . . . . . . . . . . . . . . . . . . . . .   125

COLLECTIONS, COLLECTORS, DEALERS AND AUCTIONEERS . . . . . . . . . .   131

APPENDIX Ia: NOTES ON THE MATERIALS OF THE CYLINDER SEALS
by M. Sax . . . . . . . . . . . . . . . . . . . . . . . . . . . . . . . . . . . . . . . . . . . . . . . . . . . . . . . . . .   135

APPENDIX Ib: NOTES ON THE MATERIALS OF THE GREEK, ROMAN AND
LATER ENGRAVED GEMS AND AMULETS . . . . . . . . . . . . . . . . . . . . . . . . . . .   136

APPENDIX 2: EDITION OF THE CUNEIFORM TEXTS WITH NOTES
by Dr C. Walker . . . . . . . . . . . . . . . . . . . . . . . . . . . . . . . . . . . . . . . . . . . . . . . . . . . . .   136

CONCORDANCES . . . . . . . . . . . . . . . . . . . . . . . . . . . . . . . . . . . . . . . . . . . . . . . . .   139

INDEX OF MATERIALS . . . . . . . . . . . . . . . . . . . . . . . . . . . . . . . . . . . . . . . . . . . .   143

INDEX OF PROVENANCES . . . . . . . . . . . . . . . . . . . . . . . . . . . . . . . . . . . . . . . .   144

INDEX OF SUBJECTS . . . . . . . . . . . . . . . . . . . . . . . . . . . . . . . . . . . . . . . . . . . . .   144

INDEX OF INSCRIPTIONS . . . . . . . . . . . . . . . . . . . . . . . . . . . . . . . . . . . . . . . .   147

# Acknowledgements

I would first like to thank Mr John Allan of the Royal Albert Memorial Museum, Exeter for helping in so many ways and making it possible for me to catalogue the collections of cylinder seals, stamp seals, engraved gems and amulets which were bequeathed to the Museum by Lt. Colonel Leopold A.D. Montague and Dr Norman Lace Corkill.

I am especially grateful to Professor Sir John Boardman, Dr Dominique Collon, Professor David Bivar and Dr Martin Henig who have spared time to read and comment on various sections of the catalogue. Any omissions and errors, however, are my own. The photographs – the most important feature of the catalogue – were taken by Mr Robert Wilkins to whom I am greatly indebted. I am also grateful to Mr David Garner for a number of the coloured photographs and several plates in the Introduction. The materials of the cylinder seals were analysed by Mrs Margaret Sax (Appendix Ia, p.135) and some of the other stones by Dr Brian Atkins. The cuneiform inscriptions on the tablets, cone and fragments were translated by Dr Christopher Walker (Appendix 2, pp.136–8) and those on the cylinder seals by Dr Irving Finkel.

A number of other people have helped in various ways and among them I should mention: Dr James Allan, Miss Carol Andrews, Professor Margaret Boyce, Dr Pierfrancesco Callieri, Dr A.B. Chadour Sampson, Mr R. Cockburn, Dr John Curtis, Dr Stephanie Dalley, Dr Ann Gunter, Dr P.R.S. Moorey, Dr J.P. Northover, Prince Paul Odescalchi, Professor Ulrico Pannuti, Professor Asko Parpola, Dr Dimitris Plantzos, Dr Venetia Porter, Dr Julian Raby, Dr Margaret Cool Root, Miss Gertrud Seidmann, Mr Andrew Shortland, Professor Nicholas Sims-Williams, Dr Michael Still, Dr Wang Tao, Mrs Mary Whiting and Dr Erika Zwierlein-Diehl.

I am also grateful to Mrs Margaret Pickwoad and Mrs Jennifer Estcourt – Colonel Montague's grand-daughters – for giving me access to Montague family papers. Dr Ralegh Radford, Professor Thurstan Shaw and the late Professor Martyn Jope also kindly shared their reminiscences of Colonel Montague with me. Dr Guy Corkill filled in many details of his father's life and activities.

The funding of the catalogue was provided by the National Heritage Memorial Fund as part of its Heritage Lottery Fund grant to Exeter City Museums for the re-display, conservation and documentation of its collections of Ethnography and Mediterranean Antiquities.

*Opposite*: **1** Marble, **2** Limestone, **4** Lapis lazuli, **7** Sparry calcite (translucent white), **10** Shell, **16** Chlorite (black & pale green), **19** Serpentinite (black & brown), **23** Cornelian, **24** Chalcedony, **28** Bronze, **29** Chalcedony, **30** Glass, **33** Glass, **36** Rock crystal, **41** Glass, **45** Cornelian, **47** Jasper (mottled), **48** Heliotrope/bloodstone (green jasper with small red flecks), **54** Obsidian, **79** Garnet (var. almandine), **83** Sardonyx (three-layered), **84** Heliotrope/bloodstone, **86** Glass (imitating layered agate), **91a** Faience, **97** Agate (layered or 'eyed')

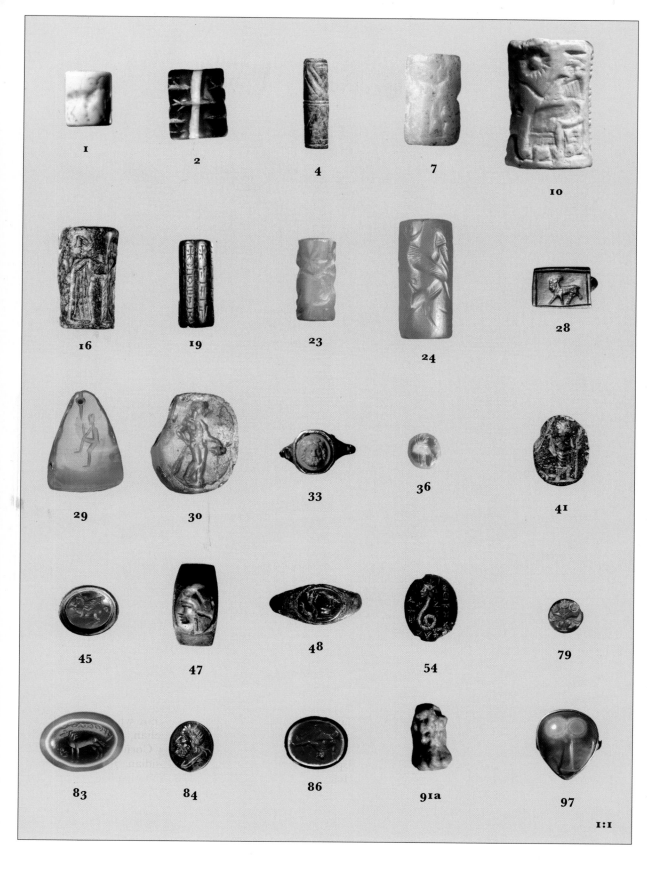

I

2

4

7

10

16

19

23

24

28

29

30

33

36

41

45

47

48

54

79

83

84

86

91a

97

1:1

# Introduction

The collection of about one hundred cylinder seals, engraved gems and amulets at the Royal Albert Memorial Museum, Exeter consists almost entirely of the bequests made by two benefactors – Lt.Col. L.A.D. Montague in 1946 and Dr N.L. Corkill in 1966. The two collections complement each other well and together they illustrate the long history of seal and gem engraving from about 3000 BC to the 19th century AD.

The seals and engraved gems described in this catalogue come mainly from the Ancient Near East (**1–29**), the Classical World (**30–65**), and the Sassanian empire (**66–83**); there are a few modern gems (**84–6**), and the amulets and miscellaneous objects (**87–101**) are typical of examples found all round the Mediterranean and in the Near East. Seven Roman engraved gems (**55–61**) found on sites in Exeter and elsewhere in Devon have been included in the catalogue although they do not form part of the Montague or Corkill bequests. These gems entered the Museum at various times and have already been published by Dr Martin Henig.

LT. COLONEL LEOPOLD AGAR DENYS MONTAGUE VD, JP, FRNS (1861–1940)
Leopold Montague (**pl.a**) was born in Pennsylvania, Exeter on 9 January 1861, and was the only son of Arthur Montague of Penton, Crediton, near Exeter. He went to Clifton College and at seventeen joined the 1st Rifle Volunteers. He later served with the Sherwood Foresters but left the regular army to rejoin the Volunteers in 1883 as Captain of the Crediton Company. During the First World War he trained recruits for home defence and retired from the army with the rank of Lieutenant Colonel. In 1886 he married Miss Amy Lind, daughter of Lt.Col. J.B. Lind. Throughout his life he played a prominent part in local affairs – military, archaeological, historical and charitable. Montague died at Penton, Crediton aged 79 on 16 April 1940.[1]

In 1946 Montague's collection of about 801 antiquities entered the Royal Albert Memorial Museum, and was then followed in 1953 by his large ethnographical collection. The antiquities are mostly Greek, Roman, Ancient Near Eastern and Egyptian; besides the engraved gems and amulets, there are ancient lamps, terracottas and bronzes. His important coin collection was sold soon after his death. Montague acquired objects for his collection over many years from dealers, auction houses, friends, and other collectors (see pp.131–3). A number of his antiquities had originally been in well-known 18th and 19th century collections. He was in frequent correspondence with the British Museum, seeking advice and opinions on antiquities, and a number of letters written to him by well-known scholars have survived.

Montague was on the committee of the Devon Archaeological Exploration Society and also a leading member of the Diocesan Architectural and Archaeological Society; he was elected a member of the Royal Numismatic Society in 1888 and joined the Society for Roman Studies. He played an important role in the excavations of Roman Exeter and from 1934 was on the Exeter Excavation Committee. The contributions he made to the Reports of the Committee

**Pl.a.** Lt. Colonel L.A.D. Montague in his drawing-room, ca.1900. (Courtesy of Mrs Margaret Pickwoad)

are mostly illustrated by him and appeared in the *Proceedings of the Devon Archaeological Exploration Society*.[2]

Montague wrote on a variety of subjects – ethnographical, historical and archaeological – and he often illustrated the articles himself with line drawings. His best-known publication is *Weapons and Implements of Savage Races (Australia, Oceania and Africa), fully illustrated by the author from specimens mostly in his collection* (1921). He wrote *The Official Guide to Crediton (North Devon)* (1925) and during the 1930s was a frequent contributor to the *Devon and Cornwall Notes and Queries* as well as to local papers on subjects of local historic and archaeological interest. He continued to take an interest in antiquarian matters until the end of his life and even played a small part in the extraordinary and fascinating story of the Crediton helmet as told by Claude Blair.[3] When it was first suggested in the *Western Morning News* on 3 January 1940 that the original mid 16th century helmet in Crediton church had been replaced by a fake, Montague replied on 8 January that he had first seen the helmet in the church in 1878 in its original 'red and rusty state', but that when he saw it sometime later it had been 'blackened over and "done up"' in what struck him as an 'injudicious way.'

lace, but when a plainer kind of dress is needed this detail might be altogether omitted. Such a model as this may be adapted to a semi-evening gown or to a useful serge—it is really only a matter of arranging trimmings and making a few changes in the opening at the neck and the length of sleeves.

Another version of the tunic is given in the second example, where plain and striped fabrics are combined. It will be noted that the seams of the under-skirt have lines of stitching on the right side; the stripes in groups were not very strongly defined in the cloth, and showed a glint of mauve, grey, and green upon a greenish-grey ground.

Braiding in narrow lines of black is applied to the well-cut coat; the vest is of a dull mauve cloth with tiny lines of black at the edge, and buttons covered with black silk crochet; the revers of dull green are trimmed with fine braiding. These tones need careful selection, and when well blended the result will be found exceedingly good. One of the colours chosen for vest or revers may be repeated on the hat, either as a full crown on a shape of soft grey felt, or in large soft puffs across the front.

**A Hint for Wet Weather.**—Dress skirts, unless very short, must be held up in bad weather, and hands are often needed for umbrella and parcels. Comfort and convenience are best served by sewing safely hooks and eyes on to the seams inside the dress skirt, the eyes about 8in. from the bottom of the skirt, pointing upwards, the hooks turned in the opposite direction and about 6in. higher up, or more, according to the amount of shortening required. Beneath a waterproof the skirt thus shortened will remain clean and dry, and it can easily be let down again when desired.—B. L. A.

## The Collector's Room.

### ROMAN FINGER-RINGS.
By LEOPOLD A. D. MONTAGUE.
(Illustrated by the Author.)
(Continued from page 1862, vol. lxxvii.)

Fig. 10 (No. 1) depicts a woman's ring which must certainly have belonged to one of the early Christians, as it bears, in intaglio, the well-known Christian emblem—a fish. The fish was so used on account of its Greek name ΙΧΘΥΣ, the letters of which form the initials of the words Ιησους Χριστος Θεου Υιος Σωτηρ "Jesus Christ, Son of God, Saviour." The seal-stone is in this case a very small carnelian (or allied gem) of a clear orange-red, oval in shape, the fish being executed in a good style of intaglio work, considering that the stone measures only .25in. lengthways. The interior diameter of the ring is .65in., the metal being silver, and the hoop is rather more ornate than usual, having sculptured shoulders. This pretty specimen was quite perfect when I purchased it, but the hoop has since been accidentally broken through being tried on by a lady, the silver having become so brittle through long interment that merely passing the ring over the finger-joint caused it to fly into several pieces. It was fortunately, however, not beyond repair. No. 2 of the same figure shows a much larger intaglio, or rather the impression made by it, formerly in the noted collection of Prince Hugo Odeschalchi. The stone is a sard, roughly measuring .8in. by .65in., and is now set in a very handsome gold ring, probably of the eighteenth century. The subject is a profile head of Jupiter, finely cut in the style of the Greek artists employed during the first half of the Roman Empire.

Before leaving the subject of intaglios I should mention the celebrated forgeries collected by Prince Poniatowsky, who had a queer mania for commissioning clever

gem-engravers to execute intaglios in the style of antique gems (usually of large size), on which he afterwards procured

**Fig. 10.**—1, Early Christian Ring, with Fish Symbol; 2, Sard Intaglio, Head of Jupiter, formerly in the Odeschalchi Collection; 3, Head of Jupiter in Turquoise (reset).

the forgery of the signatures of Greek artists, both known and imaginary. Poniatowsky collected an immense number of such bogus antiques, apparently with the sole object of posing as the possessor of a unique collection; but when he died, the fraud having become known, his collection was sold at an absurdly low price, and the specimens found their way into every part of the world, to be the occasion of much subsequent dishonesty. Cameo rings are considerably rarer than intaglios, and have been forged to an even

**Fig. 11.**—Two Roman Key Finger-rings, from Lewes and Eastcheap (London).

greater extent. The genuine examples were usually cut on stones having differently coloured layers, such as the onyx

and sardonyx; but the cheaper forgeries are sometimes made of various stones carefully stuck together. Thus a profile head, either cut from a thin white stone or even of moulded composition, may be cemented to a dark stone, in imitation of an onyx, and so on. Other forgeries are cut from shells (never used by the ancients for this purpose), and of course the best class are made of the genuine stone, and are often the work of Italian and other artists of great talent; so there are pitfalls in all directions. A beautiful ring in my possession has an exquisite facing head of Jupiter, of turquoise, cut in the cameo style (Fig. 10, No. 3), probably by a Greek artist during the early Roman Empire; but as the stone has been reset in gold (apparently about a century ago) there is nothing to prove its antiquity, although it has every appearance of authenticity, and was purchased with a guarantee.

In conclusion, I will describe two rings of a type occasionally found in Britain, which were no doubt considered both useful and ornamental being a combination of finger-ring and key, the latter probably opening the small casket in which the Roman owner kept his jewellery, &c. These rings are usually made of bronze, and are generally of the pattern represented by the three drawings of a specimen found at Lewes, Sussex, seen at the top of Fig. 11. The lock which this key opened was of the sliding-bolt pattern, the wards of the key fitting into holes in the bolt itself, by means of a narrow slot (usually forming two right-angles near the middle) cut in the lock-plate. This was the old Roman pattern, coming down from the earliest times; but at some period during the Empire the modern style of lock was invented or introduced, the slot being replaced by a keyhole in which the key turned, and the key even made with a hollow barrel, as in the present day. Such Roman rings are rare, but the second ring-key shown in Fig. 11 is on this principle, proving that it was known in Britain during the Roman occupation, the specimen having been found in the course of excavations made at Eastcheap, London. The ring is .7in. in interior diameter, and the key, being at right-angles to the hoop, lies flat on the finger when the ring is worn, thus avoiding an inconvenient projection. Roman ring-keys are worth from 5s. to 10s., according to preservation and pattern.

**A Relic of the Crusades.**—A very interesting show-case has been installed in the Musée de Cluny at Paris, constituting the history of the crucifix in art from the sixth to the eighteenth century. The pieces shown make it possible to follow the aspects under which the Crucifixion has been represented for twelve hundred years. Among other examples is that of a cross which belonged to a soldier of the First Crusade, and which was found on the site of a battlefield in Palestine.

**An Ancient Coin-die.**—While ancient coins and medals are numerous, the only genuine antique die known from which a coin could be made seems to be that found at Tel El Athrib, Egypt, in 1904. According to Science Siftings Professor C. Zenghelis reports that this is of bronze, 2½in. high and 6oz. in weight, dates from 430 to 322 B.C., and the base is engraved with the owl of the Athenian tetradrachma pieces. The alloy seems to have consisted of about 75 per cent. of copper and 25 of tin. The die is evidence of great skill in working metals.

**Sunderland Pottery.**—To judge by the quantity of Sunderland pottery that has survived until the present time, it must have been turned out in vast quantities—at least, that appealing to sailors. Jugs and bowls were especial favourites, and it is no uncommon thing to find in some houses at the present time whole sets of both "lustred" in pink. Sometimes the jugs are named and dated, when they constitute prizes to the collector, and are priced accordingly; at others they bear quaint verses, and crude pictures of favourite ships or yachts of the period. Scott Brothers, who flourished in the declining years of the eighteenth century, were prolific makers, as were also Dixon and Co. Then there are some very good Sunderland pieces of lustred ware that bear a mark something like a large asterisk, and that I have been unable to allocate to any factory. Forgeries are, however, extremely numerous, and collectors need to buy very carefully.—W.

**Pl.b.** Page from *The Bazaar, Exchange and Mart*, 4 January 1908, p.66, with Montague's column, 'The Collector's Room' (see **32–3, 46**). (Photo: The Bodleian Library, University of Oxford; shelfmark: N.23231.c.1)

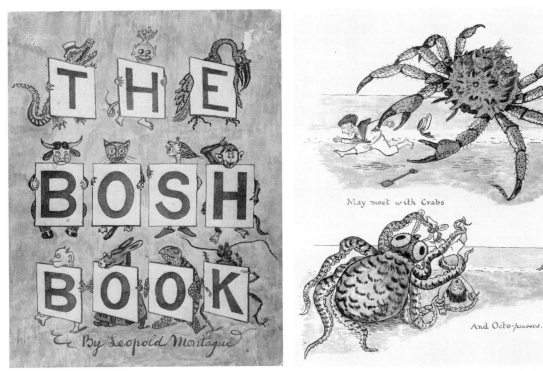

**Pl.c.** Title page of Montague's book of verse for children, *The Bosh Book* (unpublished), and the page illustrating 'The Dangers of the Deep'. (Courtesy of Mrs Margaret Pickwoad)

For many years he was on the staff of *Bazaar, the Exchange and Mart* and regularly wrote a column entitled 'The Collector's Room' in which he describes and illustrates antiquities belonging to himself and others. The column was entertaining, informative, and imaginative – but sometimes, in the light of present knowledge, not entirely accurate. Not only were the objects put into a wide context, but Montague often provides such practical details as the purchase price, value and provenance of a piece. Many of the engraved gems in the present catalogue were described and illustrated by him in *Bazaar* between 30 November 1906 and 16 October 1914 (**pl.b**).

Montague compiled a numbered typescript catalogue of his antiquities[4] which gives a brief description of each object, usually with details of provenance, price and references (if any) to his column in *Bazaar* or elsewhere. Provenances are not always certain and information (which was often passed on to Montague by dealers) is sometimes incomplete. There is no mention, for example, that the four gems from Dalmatia (**37–8,40,45**) had once been in the collection of Sir Arthur Evans.[5] A number of Evans's gems had been sold by auction at the beginning of the century, but Evans was not usually identified in the catalogues as the seller. In any case, at the time Montague purchased them – presumably in about 1907 (the year they appear in *Bazaar*) – Evans had not yet become so well-known and therefore this information might not have been considered significant. Like many of Evans's gems, they are displayed on blue velvet boards with a red sealing wax impression and a small label written by Evans himself (see back cover). (Impressions of two of the gems are also among those Evans made to record his collection (now mostly dispersed) in the Ashmolean Museum, Oxford.)

**Pl.d.** An oak chest carved by Montague. (Courtesy of Mrs Margaret Pickwoad)

**Pl.e.** Detail of the right-hand panel of the chest
(**pl.d**) showing a sphinx (cf. the cylinder seal,
**25**)

Besides building his collections and following his scholarly pursuits, Montague seems to have had the time and means, like many of his Victorian contemporaries, to pursue a variety of wide-ranging interests and hobbies. He wrote quite a number of plays which were performed on the stage – the best known was *Browne with an E*. An unpublished book of cautionary tales produced for his children, *The Bosh Book* has fine coloured illustrations and is written in rhyming verse, rather in the style of Hilaire Belloc (**pl.c**). Montague was also an accomplished wood-carver and a number of pieces of furniture are decorated with his carvings; some show scenes satirizing contemporary political figures or local characters of his acquaintance, others have motifs inspired by his gems or coins (**pls.d–e**).

Montague gives the impression of having been an extremely talented, well-informed, artistic and versatile individual who also possessed a great sense of humour and charm. He is remembered with affection not only by his grand-daughters but by a number of distinguished archaeologists: Dr Ralegh Radford was for some years on the Committee of the Devon Archaeological Exploration Society and worked with him on the Exeter excavations; the late Professor Martyn Jope remembered how Montague helped in many ways when he and the late Professor R.G. Goodchild carried on the excavations at Roman Topsham in the late 1930s; and it was Montague who fed Professor Thurstan Shaw's growing interest in archaeology – as a boy he often visited Montague's museum-like house and was fascinated to hear about the collections of antiquities and ethnographical objects.

## DR NORMAN LACE CORKILL MM, MD, CMG (1898–1966)

Norman Lace Corkill (**pl.f**) was born in Liverpool on 11 June 1898. His parents, William Lace Corkill and Bessie Furness (née Jewell), had emigrated to Liverpool from the Isle of Man. He was educated at the Liverpool Institute and then at the outbreak of the First World War he enlisted in the army. He was discharged after a year when it was discovered he was under age but he immediately rejoined a different Regiment (the King's Liverpool Regiment) and served from 1915–19. He was awarded the Military Medal in 1918.

After the war he travelled round the world as a ship's purser before attending Liverpool University in the late 1920s to study medicine. While at medical school he diagnosed a case of bubonic plague – the first to be recognized in Britain since the Black Death. He was later to have a distinguished medical career both abroad and in England. He published books and articles on ophiology and tropical medicine, for example: *Snakes and Snake Bite in Iraq* (1932) and *The Feeding of Sudanese Infants* (1946).

From 1927–30 Corkill was appointed to the Iraq Health Service as Professor of Zoology at the Royal College of Medicine, Iraq, and Civil Staff Surgeon in Baghdad. It was during these three years that he acquired his seals and other antiquities (see below). He met Max Mallowan and Agatha Christie in Iraq and it is said that the three of them would sometimes meet at the end of the day to discuss archaeology, novel writing and medicine. After returning to England in 1930 he married Phyllis Rosalie White Lavis.

Corkill spent the years from 1930–46 in the Sudan Medical Service. He was first in Nubia Province and then became Assistant Director based in Khartoum in 1938. During World War II, as Lieutenant Colonel from 1940–44 in the R.A.M.C., he trained and commanded a field hospital of the Sudan Defence Force during the campaign against Rommel in the western desert and was awarded the Order of the Nile. After the war he returned to Liverpool University where he became reader in the School of Tropical Medicine from 1946–48.

From 1948 on he took short posts abroad as Quarantine Expert in Saudi Arabia (1948–50), Health Adviser in the Aden Protectorate (1951–61), and lastly, after retirement, he was

**Pl.f.** Dr N.L. Corkill in Arab dress (Iraqi style).
(Courtesy of Dr Guy Corkill)

appointed Nutritionist with WHO in Tehran from 1962–63. During his tour in Saudi Arabia he visited Mecca in disguise and was the first person to cross the Rub Al Kali Desert by Landrover; St John Philby had crossed it before by camel. He had retired to Bude in Cornwall by 1961 and on 13 December he wrote to Dr Blackie, the Curator of the Royal Albert Memorial Museum, Exeter, offering to leave the museum his collection of 'Sumerian and Sudanese Antiquities'. (His herpetological collection was given to the Tripoli Museum after the war and may still be there.) He died in Bude on 26 September 1966.[6]

The seals and other antiquities from Iraq bequeathed by Dr Corkill to the Royal Albert Memorial Museum, Exeter in 1966 had been acquired by him between 1927 and 1930.[7] The objects from Iraq with cuneiform inscriptions were described or in some cases translated by C.J. Gadd in 1930.[8] Dr Christopher Walker of the British Museum has now revised the dating of the objects (Appendix 2, pp.136–8: Corkill nos.M.1, M.15 (**pl.g**), T.1–4, T.7 (**pl.h**)).

According to Dr Corkill's list of antiquities from Iraq, the cylinder seals, the Sassanian seals and most of the other antiquities had been acquired by him in Nasriyeh in 1927 and were said to have come from 'Lagash (Telloh)?'.

Excavations made in 1973 have now revealed that modern Tello (or Tell Luh), 30 miles north of Nasriyeh, is the site of ancient Girsu, and not ancient Lagash (which is at Al Hiba) as had been previously thought.[9] These two sites, however, are not far from each other in southeast Iraq between the Tigris and the Euphrates; both were in the city-state of Lagash.

**Pl.g.** Cone (M.15) with cuneiform inscription, mentioning Gudea the governor of Lagash (ca.2141–2122 BC). Possibly from Lagash Province. (See Appendix 2, p.136.)

**Pl.h.** Clay envelope (T.7) with a tablet still inside it. The envelope has both a cuneiform inscription and cylinder seal impression. Possibly from Umma, 2034 BC. (See Appendix 2, p.137.)

Three of the inscribed objects bought in Nasriyeh in 1927 (the limestone fragment (M.1), the cone (**pl.g** (M.15)) and a brick (M.20, not located, see p.138) mention the famous *ensi* or governor of Lagash, Gudea (ca.2141–2122 BC). Gudea rebuilt fifteen temples in Girsu (Tello) including the temple of Ningirsu, the city god mentioned on the cone (**pl.g** (M.15)).[10] Although there is some uncertainty over the provenance of the antiquities, these three inscribed objects almost certainly come from Tello. This suggests that Tello could also be the provenance for the Corkill cylinder seals and other objects – or at least some of them. In 1927, however, when Dr Corkill acquired the objects in Nasriyeh, excavations were being carried out at Ur. Nasriyeh is very close to Ur and the possibility that some of the objects might have originally come from Ur should not be excluded.[11]

# NOTES

1. See obituaries, funeral notices and bequests in the *Express and Echo*, 18/4/40, 22/4/40, 16/7/40; *Western Morning News*, 18/4/40, 22/4/40, 17/7/40. In the *Proceedings of the Royal Numismatic Society* ser.6, 11, 1941, p.11 it is noted that Montague was elected a member in 1888, was the author of a book on the Romans and was a well-known member of the staff of *Bazaar*. (Information on Montague from 1930 onwards is held in the Burnett Morris Index in Exeter Public Library.)

2. *Proceedings of the Devon Archaeological Exploration Society* 1–3:

1 (1929–32) – 'Exeter Excavations 1931' (with E. Montgomerie-Neilson) pp.121–42.

2 (1933–36) – pt.ii 'Report on the Excavations, 1932–3' (with E. Montgomerie-Neilson) pp.72–83; pt.iii 'Description of the Finds, 1932–3' (with E. Montgomerie-Neilson) pp.84–109.

'Coin found in Section 4', 'Trial Trenches in St. John's School', pp.187–8 (in 'Excavations in St. John's School' p.184ff.); 'Romano-British Midden in Exeter' pp.188–90.

'Romano-British Antiquities found at Topsham' pp.200–6.

'Roman Remains in the Cathedral Close, Exeter' pp.225–6; 'The Finds' pp.231–7.

3 (1937–47) – 'Finds from Topsham' pp.11–17, 'Roman Coins found at Topsham' pp.20–1 (in 'The Roman Site at Topsham' p.6ff.).

'The Finds' pp.70–9 (in 'A Romano-British Building at Topsham' (1938) p.67ff.).

'Potters' Stamps' pp.83–5 (in 'The Discovery of Roman Remains at the Corner of Fore Street–Market Street – Exeter').

'Small Objects' pp.139–41 (in 'Report on the Excavations of the Palace Gardens' p.136ff. which appeared posthumously in 1946 with C.A. Ralegh Radford and the late P. Morris).

3. See Claude Blair, 'Crediton: The Story of Two Helmets', *Studies in European Arms and Armor. The C.O. von Kienbusch Collection in the Philadelphia Museum of Art* (1992) pp.152–83; esp. pp.156–8.

4. A copy of Montague's typescript catalogue is in the RAM Museum, Exeter.

5. My attention was drawn to these four gems by Dr M. Henig in time to include them as an Addendum in S.E. Hoey Middleton, *Engraved Gems from Dalmatia from the Collections of Sir John Gardner Wilkinson and Sir Arthur Evans in Harrow School, at Oxford and elsewhere* (1991) (abbr. *Dalmatian Gems*).

6. See *Who was Who*, 1961–1970; and a personal communication from his son, Guy Corkill, 15 March 1993.

7. A few other antiquities acquired later by Corkill in the Sudan were also left to the RAM Museum, Exeter.

8. Corkill's lists and notes on the antiquities written by C.J. Gadd are in the RAM Museum, Exeter.

9. G. Roux, *Ancient Iraq* (2nd ed. 1980) pp.123, 413 (n.1–2) & map pp.472–9 (Sumer and Akkad).

10. See Appendix 2, p.136 and **pl.g**; G. Roux, *op.cit*, pp.158–60.

11. Six tablets (T.1–6) acquired by Corkill in Baghdad in 1929 are listed as coming from 'Kish?' – an unlikely provenance as some of the tablets are dated according to the Ur III calendar and so these probably do come from Ur. (See Appendix 2, p.138 and Corkill's letter of 18/12/61 to the Curator of the Museum and his list of antiquities.)

# Ringstone typology

Curved surfaces (Types A-C)

Depth of curve:

A          B          C

Profiles:

1          2          3          4

5          6          7          8

Flat surfaces (Type F)

Profiles:

1          2          3          4

5          6          7          8

# Sassanian stamp-seal shapes

Domes:

Ellipsoids:

# NOTES ON THE CATALOGUE ENTRIES

Information on each object (cylinder seal, engraved gem or amulet) in the catalogue is given in the following order:

## 1. LOCATION
The present catalogue number is followed by the RAM Museum, Exeter accession number, and then by any other numbers:
Montague collection typescript catalogue number and page (Montague no..., p... ).
Corkill collection number (Corkill, S.1, M.1, T.1 etc.) which appears on lists, labels and in his correspondence. (S. = Seal, M. = Miscellaneous, T. = Tablet).
Any relevant correspondence about the object is noted.

## 2. PROVENANCE
'Ex coll.[ection]', 'acquired from', 'bought' etc. and where known the date and/or price is given.
Sometimes the find spot or place of acquisition is uncertain: 'probably from...', 'From Tello(?)' etc.

## 3. MATERIAL AND DESCRIPTION OF THE OBJECT
After naming the object – '**Cylinder Seal**', '**Ringstone**' etc. – a description of its material is given and remarks on its condition. The term 'cornelian' rather than 'sard' is generally used. In some cases Montague's or Corkill's description of the material is added in inverted commas. It is noted when stones were tested or analysed.

## 4. MEASUREMENTS AND SHAPE
(All measurements are given to the nearest 0.5mm.)
**Cylinder seal:** Height and width (and sometimes diameter of perforation) followed, if necessary, by a description of its shape ('slightly concave' etc.) and remarks on its condition.

**Stamp seal:** Height and width of seal at the widest point (and sometimes diameter of perforation) followed by the length and breadth of the intaglio face and its shape ('convex' etc.).

**Scaraboid, tabloid, scarab:** Length, breadth and depth.

**Intaglio, ring** (metal ring with intaglio on bezel): Height, width and depth of bezel (intaglio face), followed by the height and width of the ring measured externally; and where relevant the shape and dimensions of the hoop.

**Ringstone:** Length, breadth and depth. If the gem has a bevelled edge and the intaglio face is smaller than the overall size both sets of measurements are given (for shapes F.2,3,4,8). (Where a ringstone is mounted in a ring it is not possible to give its depth if the back of the bezel is filled in.)
Mount (ring): height (inc. ringstone) and width are measured externally and type of hoop described.
Intagli from Evans's collection are mounted on blue velvet boards with a sealing wax impression and handwritten label.

**Lead sealing:** Overall measurements, then length and breadth of impressed surface or surfaces.

**Stamp seals** (Sassanian): dome – height, width at widest point and diameter of the intaglio face; ellipsoid – height, both widths at widest point, the diameter of the perforation and length and breadth of the intaglio face.

**Amulets:** Height, width and, where relevant, depth.

**Shape:** For ringstones the code follows the one used by M. Henig (after J. Boardman and E. Zwierlein-Diehl) in *Britain* and *Sa'd*. (For Sassanian ringstones A.D.H. Bivar's *LondonSass* code is also given.) For Sassanian stamp seals see chart opposite.

**Scale:** Scales vary and are given with each illustration.

## 5. PUBLICATIONS
A list of publications in which the objects are described or mentioned is given with references to illustrations (if any).

## 6. DESCRIPTION OF AN ENGRAVED MOTIF
This is given as the intaglio appears in impression (except in the case of cameos and some amulets).

## 7. ENGRAVING TECHNIQUE AND STYLE
Where possible the engraving technique, style and tools used are described. For Roman ringstones Dr M. Maaskant-Kleibrink's *Hague* catalogue has often been used as a guide (see p.59ff.).

## 8. GENERAL REMARKS ON THE OBJECT AND/OR MOTIF

## 9. PARALLELS FOR THE OBJECT, OR MOTIF AND STYLE
Parallels for the object and the motif and/or style on gems, coins or other objects are given where possible.

## 10. DATE
Approximate dates are given where possible, mainly based on dated examples of similar style in other collections, or other evidence.

# Catalogue

## I ANCIENT NEAR EASTERN CYLINDER SEALS AND STAMP SEALS: (1–29)

Stamp seals (or seal-like stamps) made of stone or baked clay with a knob on the back have been found on sites in Turkey and Syria and date from the 7th and 6th millennia BC. It seems likely that they were used for stamping goods, textiles or perhaps bread because no clay sealings from this early period have survived. The earliest clay sealings found so far come from sites in Turkey and northern Iraq and date back to the late 5th millennium BC. It is also at this time that stone seals with perforations appear which suggests that they could have been worn and so have had a personal significance.

By the 4th millennium (ca.3500 BC) the first cylinder seals were being made in southern Iraq and south-western Iran and were to replace the early stamp seals in that area by the beginning of the 3rd millennium although stamp seals continued to be used, often alongside cylinder seals, in other areas, particularly Turkey. Cylinder seals developed at the same time as writing, and cuneiform inscriptions on clay are often accompanied by cylinder seal impressions. Cylinder seals continued in use for over three thousand years but when alphabets were invented and clay was less often used to write on, stamp seals were re-introduced in the 1st millennium BC after a gap of about two thousand years (**27**). By the time of the fall of the Achaemenid Persian empire (539 BC–331 BC) cuneiform was no longer used and cylinder seals became obsolete.

Cylinder seals were usually carved in *intaglio* (as were stamp seals) and were rolled across the clay to leave a continuous impression of the design in relief. The design was usually engraved in reverse on the stone because it was meant to be seen as it appears on the impression – this is especially evident where there is an inscription (although in the 1st millennium BC most inscriptions were cut to be read from the stone and are therefore reversed on the impression). Most cylinder seals were perforated longitudinally so they could be worn by the owner and therefore, besides being functional, had a decorative and probably amuletic value.

There were three main categories of seals: personal, official and votive. They were used like signatures on the clay to authenticate documents, for identification and also to secure doors and containers. They could cover large surfaces much more effectively than stamp seals and so were especially suited to sealing large areas on clay balls, envelopes or tablets which gave details of consignments of goods, agreements or identified ownership. The clay balls were hollow and actually contained tokens identifying numbers and types of goods. Tablets are often encased in clay envelopes sealed by witnesses to a transaction. These have often been broken open to reveal the contents but in the Corkill collection an intact envelope, possibly from Umma, dated to 2034 BC, has its tablet still enclosed inside it. This envelope was first impressed all over with the cylinder seal of Nin-MAR.KI-ka, the 'libator', and then on top of this was written a record of the votive offerings of animals made to the gods, Shara and Gula, on behalf of the king of Ur (Shu-Suen) by Akalla, the governor of Umma (**pl.h** (T.7)).[12]

For each historical period and geographical area the style of engraving and iconography is quite distinctive. The use of certain stones also was confined almost exclusively to particular periods and groups of cylinders. This probably reflects variations in trade patterns as well as the availability of raw materials. Earlier seals were as a rule made in relatively soft stones but by the second half of the 2nd millennium BC, quartz, which was much harder to work, was occasionally used. (For the materials see Appendix Ia, p.135.) The more frequent use of quartz ($SiO_2$ – which includes cornelian, chalcedony and jasper) seems to have coincided with technical advances in engraving technique, improved materials and with use of a cutting wheel on a lathe. Various methods were used for engraving – micro-chipping, filing, drilling and wheel cutting. It was once thought that the cutting wheel (adapted from the vertically held bow-drill) was used as early as the 4th millennium BC but recent studies of quartz seals with a scanning electron microscope have suggested that this innovation probably did not take place until the second millennium BC.[13]

Twenty Ancient Near Eastern seals entered the Royal Albert Memorial Museum in 1966 as part of the Dr Norman Lace Corkill bequest (**1–7,9–18,22–3,26**), eight as part of the Lt.Col. Leopold A.D. Montague bequest in 1946 (**8,19–21,24–5,27–9**) and one (**11**) was acquired separately in 1933. They correspond in material and iconography to seals in the British Museum and other large collections. Examples from most periods are represented here – from the early seals of the Jemdet Nasr Period, pre 3000 BC (**1–3**) to the Neo-Babylonian period of about 9th–7th century BC when cylinder seals and stamp seals were being used concurrently (**23–5,27**). A few are interesting and unusual: the Early Dynastic or Akkadian fossil shell seal (**6**); the Old Babylonian seal with inscription (**19**); and two fine quality Neo-Babylonian seals (**24–5**).

For a comprehensive survey of cylinder seals see: D. Collon, *First Impressions* (1987) (abbr. *FI*); idem, *Near Eastern Seals* (1990) (which includes stamp seals); D.J. Wiseman, *Catalogue of the Western Asiatic Seals in the British Museum . . .* 1 (1962), D. Collon, 2 (1982), 3 (1986) (abbr. *LondonWA* 1–3); B. Buchanan, *Catalogue of the Ancient Near Eastern Seals in the Ashmolean Museum* 1 (abbr. *OxfordANE* 1).

## NOTES

[12.] See reading for **pl.h** (T.7), Appendix 2, p.137.
[13.] For a discussion see M. Sax & N.D. Meeks, 'The Introduction of Wheel Cutting as a Technique for Engraving Cylinder Seals: Its Distinction from Filing' *Iraq* 56 (1994) pp.153–66; idem, 'Methods of Engraving Mesopotamian Quartz Cylinder Seals' *Archaeometry* 37, 1 (1995) pp.25–36.

**1** (see also frontispiece)                                                3:2

**1**  86/1966 (Corkill, S.19)
From Tello(?)

**Cylinder seal**, white marble.
15 × 12mm

A *Horned animal* facing left, a temple or shrine
and a conical reed hut; a plant(?) or vessel(?)
in the field.

This cylinder and **2–3** belong to the Jemdet
Nasr group which is dated to before 3000 BC.
These are contemporary with Uruk seals but are
stylistically different. Jemdet Nasr seals are
found mostly in the Diyala region, north east of
Baghdad (frequently on temple sites), and also in
Syria. Limestone or marble, which are relatively
soft materials (H=3) and easy to work, were
commonly used for cylinders at this early date
and continued to be used in the Early Dynastic
periods (**5,7**). Jemdet Nasr seals are usually
small, squat and often made in dark stone (**2**).
The engraving here has been done primarily
with a drill (a large round drill for the body, and
smaller drill for the eyes and joints) and the finer
lines with hand-held tools such as gravers and
perhaps files. (Recent research suggests that the
cutting wheel was not used for engraving seals
until the 2nd millennium BC – see remarks p.2,
& note 13.)
    On Jemdet Nasr seals horned animals
frequently appear beside a temple facade and
there are often small objects in the field,
sometimes distinguishable as vessels or plants.
The simple reed hut on this seal seems unusual
but is of a type which can still be seen in the
marshes of Iraq today, used to house both men
and animals. (Compare a similar but rather more
elaborate reed building on the Early Sumerian
alabaster trough from Uruk of about the same
date: E. Strommenger, *The Art of Mesopotamia*

(1964), pl.23 (BM 120000) pp.384–5 (= *GMA*,
no.623).)
    Although there is little evidence for the actual
use of these early seals as no impressions have
been found on Diyala sites, it has been suggested
that they were used for administrative purposes
connected with shrines or temples, and/or
possibly for sealing consignments of goods for
sending elsewhere. This seal, therefore, might
have belonged to an official or office dealing with
grain production and storage, and/or animal
husbandry. (Frankfort thought that these
cylinders might have been dedicatory objects or
amulets rather than seals.) (For seals of this
period see *FI*, pp.12–19,187; Jemdet Nasr seals
pp.15–19.)

For other Jemdet Nasr seals of this type, see:

*OxfordANE* 1, no.21 – mottled light and dark
    brown limestone (3.5 × 2.85cm); four horned
    animals beside a shrine; their bodies shown
    by three deep drill holes and smaller ones for
    joints; six drill holes with appendages in the
    field.
*LondonWA* 1, pl.5e (= *FI*, no.28, p.18) – gypsum
    (4.45 × 3.85cm); horned animals and others
    in front of a temple facade; the heads of the
    animals are shown as three small drill holes
    joined by three narrow lines, as on the Exeter
    seal.
    pl.5a (= *FI*, no.921) – grey-green stone (1.95 ×
    2.95cm); bodies are shown by three drill holes
    as on the Exeter seal.
*Yale*, nos.162–8 – marble or limestone; horned
    animals with a shrine or temple.
*Corpus*, no.22 – white marble (3.7 × 3.3cm); two
    goats and shrine; vessels in the field.
*Heeramaneck*, no.1127 – two horned animals and
    shrine.

Jemdet Nasr: pre-3000 BC

 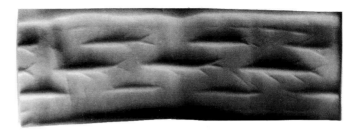

**2** (see also frontispiece)                                    3:2

**2**  86/1966 (Corkill, S.9)
From Tello(?)

**Cylinder seal**, black limestone, with vertical white vein.
19 × 14mm

*Three rows of fish* swimming in parallel lines – the top two rows to the left and the bottom row perhaps to the right; the fish in the central row are staggered between the fish in the other two.

The fish are shown by straight filed grooves. Some of the finer, pointed grooves of the tails and fins have worn away but traces of fin show the bottom row of fish swimming in the opposite direction to the other two.

It is possible that this seal could have been used by an official who dealt with fishing.

Fish and other animals often appear in rows or patterns on seals of this period, see:

Delaporte 2 (1923) pl.61.10 (A.6) – white marble (2.1 × 1.7cm) 'Sumer and Akkad'; a close parallel; the middle row of fish swim in the opposite direction to the other two.
*OxfordANE* 1, no.49 – pink marble mottled white (2.7 × 2.2cm); two rows of fish in registers; very similar to the Exeter seal. From Jemdet Nasr. (Also no.50)
*Malter 58* (1994), no.185 – cream and white marble or calcite; six rows of fish; each row swimming in the opposite direction to the last.

Jemdet Nasr: pre-3000 BC

**3**                                              3:2

**3**  86/1966 (Corkill, S.13)
From Tello(?)

**Cylinder seal**, white marble.
25 × 9–10mm

*An Animal with long horns and short tail* (an antelope?) facing to the right; a plant or tree(?) in the field, and a four-pointed star above.

This seal is engraved in the usual Jemdet Nasr style with hand-held tools such as files and/or gravers. The animal's body is shown as three round broad hollows. The cylinder, however, is taller and narrower than the usual Jemdet Nasr type (cf. **1–2**) and so it may date to the end of the period. Like the two close parallels listed below, this seal appears to belong to a group which seems to be transitional between the usual squat Jemdet Nasr type and the so-called 'Brocade style' cylinders (often in dark stone) from the Diyala region which are very tall and narrow and dated slightly later – that is to the beginning of the Early Dynastic I Period (2900–2750 BC).

On Brocade style cylinders, animal motifs engraved with the file are repeated to form a pattern but the animals' bodies are typically shown as two narrow parallel lines rather than the three round hollows usual on Jemdet Nasr cylinders. A typical example which can be compared is *LondonWA* 1, pl.13b (scapolite 7.5 × 1.2cm) which shows horned animals, stags and stars. Although the animals' bodies are shown

quite differently, the antlers of the stags are shown in the same way as the plant/tree(?) on the Exeter cylinder. There is no sign that the Exeter cylinder has been broken in half or cut down – otherwise the plant might have been the antlers belonging to a missing stag engraved below on a seal of Brocade style type. (For the Brocade style see also *FI*, p.24, no.59.)

The following cylinders are very similar in style and proportions to the Exeter example:

*OxfordANE* 1, no.25 – Jemdet Nasr, banded light green quartzite (24.5 × 1.1cm); antelope with four-pointed stars or birds; the animal's body shown as broad grooves.

*LondonWA* 1, pl.6h – Jemdet Nasr, marble (3.1 × 1.5cm); goat engraved in the same way, a tree, rhomb and four-pointed star. From Ur.

pl.6d – Jemdet Nasr, gypsum (3.8 × 1.2cm); similar but taller proportions.

Jemdet Nasr, probably late: about 3000 BC

**4** (see also frontispiece)        3:2

**4** 86/1966 (Corkill, S.15)
From Tello(?)

**Cylinder seal**, lapis lazuli.
25 × 6–7mm (slightly barrel-shaped)

*Two registers*: in both an identical *zig-zag pattern* of three parallel lines – a broad groove between two narrow grooves; straight parallel lines divide the registers and form a border at the top and bottom.

This belongs to a group of tall, narrow cylinder seals with geometric designs in two or three registers which are dated to the early part of the Early Dynastic III period (2600–2334 BC). The designs seem to be revivals of the earlier Jemdet Nasr period geometric seals (e.g. *OxfordANE* 1, no.66 – 'steatite'; a similar pattern on an earlier squat seal).

Examples of this later group, but generally with a more undulating design, have been found in Southern Mesopotamia, mostly at Ur, and are always in lapis lazuli (H=4–5.5) which had become common at this time – though softer materials are still extensively used (**5ff**.). Lapis lazuli is largely restricted to the third millennium BC. The seals were probably originally imported as beads (which are often barrel-shaped) but engraved locally. For geometric seals of the period see *FI*, pp.20–3 and no.52; and for lapis lazuli, D. Collon, *Near Eastern Seals* (1990) pp.32–3.

For similar geometric designs on lapis lazuli cylinders, see:

*London WA* 1, pl.10l (= *FI*, no.52) – (4.4 × 0.9cm); undulating lines in three registers.
  pl.10m – (3.4 × 1.2cm); undulating lines in two registers. From Ur.
Delaporte 2 (1923) pl.61.9 (A.3) – (2.1 × 0.7cm); three thin parallel zig-zag lines, rounded at the apex.

Early Dynastic III: about 2500 BC

**5**                                                                 3:2

**5**  86/1966 (Corkill, S.6)
From Tello(?)

**Cylinder seal**, cream/white limestone.
37 × 11–13mm (slightly barrel-shaped)

*Animals in two registers* divided by two thin parallel lines. In the upper register three animals face to the right: a rampant lion attacks a short-tailed animal (a sheep or goat?) from behind and a horned animal walks in front; behind the lion is a tree beneath a crescent moon. In the lower register is a frieze with a scorpion and two rosettes. Round drill holes in the field – one in the upper register (perhaps the sun) and five below.

The rosette design (often found in the Diyala) dates to the early part of the Early Dynastic period – the early 3rd millennium BC (e.g. *FI*, no.44). This design seems to have been revived and combined with other scenes of later date. On the Exeter cylinder it appears with the earliest type of contest scene where lions are shown attacking their prey from behind. (Later scenes show lions attacking their prey from in front and often men intervene – see example below.) The crescent is unusual at this time but later on, from the Akkadian period, it became common and was the symbol of the moon god, Sin. (For contest scenes see *FI*, pp.193–7 and no.940 for a pre-3000 BC example in a different style.)

Seals in this linear style have been found widely dispersed from the Diyala to central and southern Mesopotamia in Early Dynastic IIIA and IIIB contexts.

Compare the following cylinder seals in two registers:

*OxfordANE* I, no.133 (= *FI*, no.53) – end of the 3rd millennium BC (Early Dynastic II), lapis lazuli; an early arch and rosette design below with a later type of animal and human figure contest scene above.

 no.235 – Early Dynastic III, brown limestone; an animal contest frieze in the upper register similar to the Exeter scene.

 no.106 – Early Dynastic I (before 2750 BC), calcite and limestone; processions of animals in both registers; engraved in very similar style – especially the heads which are shown in outline.

*GMA*, no.774 – antelopes passant attacked by a rampant lion; double axe pattern below; transitional period. From Ur.

*Marcopoli*, no.63 – ED IIIA ca.2500–2334, chalk; in the lower register three animals walk towards a bush engraved in linear style very similar to those on the Exeter seal (see p.9 for this style); in the upper register is a banqueting scene.

 Early Dynastic II or III: about 2650–2500 BC

[For illustration **6** see p.8]

**6** 86/1966 (Corkill, S.1)
From Tello(?)

**Cylinder seal**, white/cream fossil shell. (confirmed by XRD analysis)
45 × 30mm

*Combat scene with rampant lions and human figures.* Several rampant animals are visible: to the left of centre a symmetrical group with two lions standing back to back – the lion on the right clearly has its paw on the neck of another animal which has its head turned back towards another smaller(?) animal. On the right a hero or god (his head missing but shoulder shown as a round drill hole) stands in profile with another (smaller?) rampant animal in front of him to the right.

The seal is in bad condition with a very weathered, ridged surface. The material of this seal, which is cut from an Upper Cretaceous fossil shell, is unusual. (Shell seals (H=3.5) were usually cut from the large columella of meso- or neogastropods.) This seal appears to have been cut from an oyster-like bivalve, probably about 80 million years old. Strata of this age occur in Northern Iraq and its environs. (See Appendix Ia, p.135.)

For other cylinders in shell see:

*Geneva* I, pl.12, no.27 – before mid 3rd millennium BC.
 pl.17, no.32 – Akkadian.

  Early Dynastic II/III: about 2750–2334 BC
   or Akkadian: 2334–2154 BC (?)

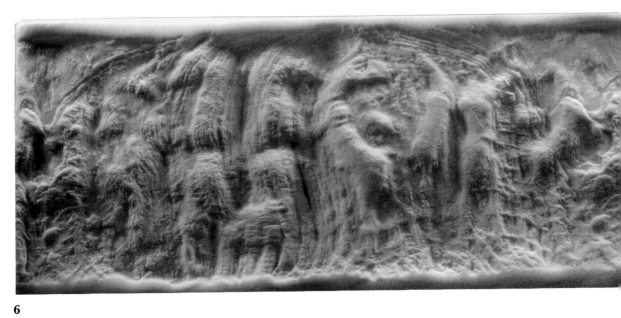

**6**

**7**  (see also frontispiece)                                                    3:2

**7**  86/1966 (Corkill, S.8)
From Tello(?)

**Cylinder seal**, sparry calcite, translucent white.
(confirmed by XRD analysis)
25 × 15mm

*Contest scene*: a hero, three rampant animals and a crescent moon above; the lion on the left has its tail in the air, the animals on either side of the hero have their heads turned back – one has a long tail and the other is probably horned. A horizontal line is cut round the centre of the seal and there are two round drill holes in the field.

This seal is rather worn. It probably belongs to the beginning of the Early Dynastic Period but may have been recut later in the Early Dynastic or in the early Akkadian period. Calcite (H=3), like limestone and marble, is a carbonate; it is easy to work.

At this time contest scenes developed from a horizontal frieze (cf. **5**) to a vertical composition with rampant animals (often crossed), heroes and bull-men (see *FI*, p.27). It has been suggested that cutting a line through a single scene on a cylinder may have been a way of cancelling the seal.

The cutting is angular but the round drill has been used for the head of the hero, the lion's eyes and the bodies of the animals.

For Early Dynastic III and early Akkadian Period contest scenes see:

*London WA* 1, pl.16e – ED III or Early Akkadian, serpentine; a hero between two animals with heads turned away and a lion on the right; a star in a crescent.

pls.17a, 21e – single scenes with a horizontal line cut through them.

*EGAZ*, abb.15 (Tehran 21) – Akkadian I ('Sumerian' group) serpentine; the same composition.

*Oxford ANE* 1, no.187 – Early Dynastic III, shell; head of hero shown as a drill hole; other drill holes in the field. From Kish.

no.208 – Early Dynastic III, alabaster; similar composition but more vertical. From Kish.

no.267 – early Akkadian, dark green serpentine; similar composition but more vertical.

*Yale*, no.307 – ED III, light brown limestone; nude hero between two antelopes attacked by a lion(?) on either side; two round drill holes in the field.

no.391 – early Akkadian, serpentine; nude hero between two antelopes attacked by lions on either side.

Early Dynastic III to early Akkadian: about
2500–2300 BC

**8**                                              3:2

**8**  5/1946.407 (Montague no.263, p.25)

**Cylinder seal**, serpentinite, black (and brown).
31 × 19mm

Publ.: *Expert* (Feb.1909) p.62, fig.1.

*Contest scene*: in the centre are two crossed rampant bulls and on the right a rampant lion with its head shown from above; on the left of the three animals a bearded hero (the head missing) wearing a belted loin-cloth, grasps the bull by the leg; on the right a bearded bull-man, wearing a belt and flat cap with chevrons, raises his right arm. In the field, horns (or a crook?), a lizard and a knife.

This belongs to the early part of the Akkadian period (ca.2300 BC) when serpentinite (H=4–6) was the most common material used for contest scenes. The style of engraving is distinctly Akkadian but the composition where the contestants form a single group with a diagonal and vertical emphasis is still Early Dynastic III –

later in the period they formed separate groups. The lion's head seen from above (though now shown rather differently) is also an Early Dynastic period feature. Some details have been lost as the cylinder is rather worn. (For Akkadian seals (2334–2193 BC) see *FI* pp.32–5, 193ff.; *London WA* 2, pp.37–8.)

Compare:

*EGAZ*, abb.49 – black and white limestone; close in style and the same composition though the bull-man on the right twists round to grapple with the lion; a lizard in the field; (Akkadian 1b group).

*London WA* 2, nos.1–3,5–6 – large serpentine seals, engraved in similar style and uninscribed; sometimes a dagger or mace in the field.

no.63 – serpentine; similar style and grouping of the three animals on the right; here the contestants form two separate groups; the lion's head is seen from above.

*Heeramaneck*, no.1170 – unfinished Akkadian jasper seal; the 'doubly recurved object' held by the hero appears to be the same as the object resembling horns on the Exeter cylinder.

Early Akkadian: about 2300 BC

**9**

3:2

**9**  86/1966 (Corkill, S.3)
From Tello(?)

**Cylinder seal**, white/cream shell.
33+ × 25–23mm (top broken off; slightly concave)

*A Vegetation god or goddess* wearing a flounced robe is seated on a wicker-work(?) throne on the left and is approached by three figures (a worshipper and/or other deities?) – all their heads are missing. Two of the approaching figures have both hands outstretched (holding offerings?), and the third carries a plough(?); the first wears a short plain thin skirt (his legs show through) and the other two wear long striped, belted robes or skirts. Branches of vegetation sprout round the throne and from the legs of the first figure.

The seal is worn and the top is broken off. Although serpentinite (**8**) was the most popular material for seals in the Akkadian period, shell was also often used (**10**). A round drill has been used to mark the shoulders of the figures. As the heads are missing it is impossible to determine whether the figures are gods or goddesses, or whether one of them is a worshipper. These scenes were popular (see *London WA* 2, p.99, nos.207–22 for variations).

For similar scenes see:

*London WA* 2, no.209 (= *FI*, no.106; *EGAZ*, abb.541 – Akkadian III) – serpentine; the goddess sits on a throne of the same type and one deity carries a plough.
    no.212 – serpentine; two deities with both hands outstretched as on the Exeter seal.
*Corpus*, no.207 E – black serpentine; three gods approach a vegetation deity, one with a plough; the same theme as the Exeter seal but engraved in a different style.

Akkadian: about 2300 BC

**10**  (see also frontispiece)

3:2

**10**  86/1966 (Corkill, S.2)
From Tello(?)

**Cylinder seal**, white/cream shell.
36 × 24–22mm (slightly concave)

*A Couchant bull* bears a winged 'gate' on its back; on the left a goddess(?) on a box-like throne holds one of the bull's horns; she has her hair looped up behind and wears a flat cap, a long fringed robe with a decorated hem, and a striped top; above them is a star or sun and crescent moon; an attendant on the right (probably male) holds a rope which is attached to the gate. Terminal, a tree.

The meaning of this scene is unclear but various theories have been put forward. The tree appears on some seals of this type and there may be an association with a vegetation god; on the other hand the 'gate' may be connected with the sun god (see *LondonWA* 2, pp.87–8, nos.178–84). The star/sun is unusual but on two cylinders from

Kish (see below) it is shown in the same way as on this cylinder. From Akkadian times onwards the crescent became the symbol of the moon god, Sin, the patron deity of Ur.

Compare similar scenes with slight variations:

*LondonWA* 2, no.178 – aragonite (shell); the god holds the bull's head (the other end of the rope or a cup is more usual).
  no.181 (= *FI*, no.107) – serpentine.
  no.182 – serpentine; a similar seated goddess(?) but she holds the rope; tree terminal.
  no.231 – serpentine; a different presentation scene but the deities wear the same fringed robes as on the Exeter seal.
*EGAZ*, abb.76 – Akkadian Ib; a different scene but engraved in very similar style with the star/sun(?) shown in the same way as on the Exeter seal; also a tree. From Kish.
*OxfordANE* 1, no.164a,b – Early Dynastic III, limestone; an animal contest but a 'star' (or sun?) as above. From Kish.

Akkadian: 2334–2193 BC

**11**

3:2

**11**  27/1933

Said to have been presented by Revd the Hon. Canon A.F. Northcote ex C.M. Doughty, the Arabian traveller and author of *Documents Epigraphiques*, but the seal described below does not correspond to the description in the Museum Accession Register.

**Cylinder seal**, chlorite, black (and brown). 28 × 13mm

*Contest scene* showing a figure (human, hero or bull-man?) with arm raised on the left of two rampant crossed lions; possibly a plant or other object below on the left of the animals and another object on the right. A crescent above in a blank panel; possibly signs of an inscription.

The cutting is linear and cursory. The figure stands to one side of the contest but as the seal is

very worn his legs are no longer visible. The lions' manes are shown as short parallel grooves. The inscription has either never existed or been erased and never been re-cut. (See *FI*, pp.120–2 for re-use of seals; pp.32–8 for Akkadian, and Post-Akkadian and Ur III seals.) The crossed animals would suggest that the seal was probably originally Early Dynastic or, more probably, Akkadian. However, taking into account that the seal is chlorite (cf. **12–16**) and the traces of an erased inscription, it is more likely to be a worn and extensively re-cut seal of the Post-Akkadian or Ur III period.

Compare:

*EGAZ*, abb.17 – a similar composition but with two more animals ('Akkadian Ia group'). From Ur.

Post-Akkadian or Ur III: about 2192–2004 BC (or possibly Early Dynastic or Akkadian: about 2600–2193 BC)

**12**                                                                                                3:2

**12**   86/1966 (Corkill, S.12)
From Tello(?)

**Cylinder seal**, black chlorite with pale green translucent phase.
24 × 9(10)mm

*Contest scene*: two naked, clean-shaven heroes grappling with a rampant lion; the figure on the left grasps the lion by its forepaws and the one on the right by its mane and tail. A standard mace terminal.

Above and below the lion's forepaws and behind its right leg objects or signs appear in the field – the remains of two lines of inscription:

ma – x
dub? – sar?

This and the following seals (**13–17**) belong to the Post-Akkadian and Ur III periods (2192–2004 BC) after the disintegration of the Akkadian empire. Whereas serpentinite (H=4–6) was very usual for Akkadian seals, chlorite (H=2.5), a softer stone, becomes the most common material from the end of the 3rd millennium BC. It seems that harder stones such as serpentinite were no longer available.

This type of composition is a development of the Akkadian contest scene and many examples were found at Ur. There is no way of distinguishing Post-Akkadian from Ur III contest scenes. Three figure compositions are now usual and two heroes are needed to combat a lion, rather than a single hero as in Akkadian times. As there is now more space the arms of the contestants (which often appear disproportionately long) are not bent at such a sharp angle as on Akkadian seals. The engraving is very often cursory with little attempt at modelling and there is not much variation in the treatment of the subject. This seal appears to have been re-cut and the objects or signs are possibly the remains of an inscription which is difficult to identify. They might give the name of the seal's owner, and his profession.

(See *FI*, pp.35–8 for Post-Akkadian and Ur III seals, p.193 for contest scenes; *LondonWA* 2, p.114, nos.244–82 for contest scenes of the Post-Akkadian and Ur III period; *GM*, pp.15–16, no.73ff.)

Compare the same scene:

*GM*, no.76 (Baghdad Mus.) – Ur III, diorite; very similar though the figures are rather more substantial; a mace terminal. From Tello. (Also no.66ff.)

*LondonWA* 2, no.246 – Post-Akkadian to Ur III, chlorite; with inscription.

no.261 – Post-Akkadian to Ur III, serpentine; erased inscription. From Ur.

*OxfordANE* 1, no.411 – Ur III, 'steatite'; figures more modelled; two columns for inscription never written.

Post-Akkadian or Ur III: 2192–2004 BC

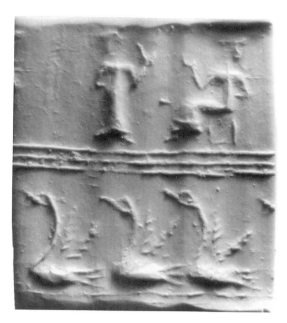

**13**

3:2

**13**   86/1966 (Corkill, S.4)
From Tello(?)

**Cylinder seal**, black chlorite with green
translucent phase.
(confirmed by XRD analysis)
52 × 10–12mm (slightly barrel-shaped)

*Scenes in two registers* divided by three
horizontal lines: in the upper register a
worshipper (or worshipping goddess?)
wearing a plain robe, with left hand raised
and the other at her waist, approaches a
figure (a goddess?) seated on a box-throne
who wears a long plain robe with double-
rolled hem and has her right hand raised;
neither appears to wear a head-dress.

Below, three geese with wings spread swim
to the left on double lines which represent
water.

This belongs to a group of Post-Akkadian seals in
two registers which have a presentation,
procession or banqueting scene in the upper
register and animals (often geese) in the lower.

Many were found in the so-called hypogeum at
Tello (*GM*, p.6, all dated by Parrot to the Ur III
period). For seals of this type see also *LondonWA* 2,
p.120; *FI*, p.36.

On this seal a single figure stands alone before
a deity without a leading or suppliant goddess (a
variation on the usual three-figure presentation
scene, cf. **14–16**). A space, though, has perhaps
been left for a third participant or the inscription;
this was later to become the rule in the Ur III
period (e.g. *LondonWA* 2, no.331 – Ur III cylinder
of this type with inscription).

Parrot makes a distinction between
'presentation' and 'intercession' scenes.
Intercession, like presentation scenes, usually have
three participants but more rarely there is only a
worshipper and a deity who can be seated or
standing. (For the two types of scene see *GM*,
pp.23–4,46–7 and remarks for **15** here.)

This seal is worn and it is not clear whether a
deity or a worshipper is shown before the seated
goddess; both appear to wear their hair looped up
behind. Identification of the figures on these
scenes is difficult as deities do not always wear
head-dresses at this time. Their plain robes, lack
of head-dresses and hair styles are typically Post-
Akkadian.

Compare:

*GM*, no.34 (Louvre AO.15481) – Ur III, shell; two registers with geese below; 'intercession' scene with two standing figures and inscription; very similar to the Exeter seal. From Tello.

no.221 (Baghdad Mus.) – Ur III, grey stone; two figure 'intercession' scene and inscription. From Tello.

*LondonWA* 2, no.287 – Post-Akkadian to Ur III, chlorite; two registers with geese below; two worshippers, both with their left hand raised and the other at waist level before a standing deity.

no.288 (= *FI*, no.113) – Post-Akkadian to Ur III, chlorite; two registers with geese below; two worshippers, one leading the other, approach a third seated figure; they wear plain robes, have the same hair style without head-dresses; very similar in style to the Exeter seal.

*OxfordANE* 1, no.441 – Ur III, 'steatite'; two figure scene: worshipping goddess before a seated goddess, with inscription.

Post-Akkadian: 2192–2112 BC

**14**                                                                3:2

**14**  86/1966 (Corkill, S.14)
From Tello(?)

**Cylinder seal**, chlorite, black (and pale green).
24 × 11mm

*Presentation scene*: a worshipper, with his right arm across his chest, is led by a deity with her left hand raised, towards a goddess standing on the right wearing a horned head-dress and holding out her right hand. All three figures wear fringed robes with double-rolled hems. Above is a crescent moon; terminal, a date palm.

This seal and **15** show characteristics of both the Post-Akkadian and Ur III periods. Presentation scenes, the most common subject on cylinder seals at this time, were to become more stereotyped in the Ur III period. For Post-Akkadian to Ur III presentation scenes see *LondonWA* 2, pp.111,124, nos.307,312–13,316. Many examples come from Tello (see *GM*, pp.23–4, nos.104–203) and see **16** here for the 'standard' Ur III presentation scene.

In the Post-Akkadian period the worshipper often holds his arm at waist level as he does on this seal (in the Ur III period he raises his hand in a gesture of deference); trees are also a common feature (in the Ur III period an inscription is usual). On the other hand the main goddess's horned head-dress and the fringed robes worn by all three figures were to become more common in the Ur III period. (The heads of the worshipper and the leading goddess are almost completely worn away so details are not visible.)

It is unusual to show the main deity standing rather than seated (though there are a number of examples from Tello, see below).

For similar scenes compare:

*FI*, no.621 – black 'lydite'; an Akkadian version of the scene.

*GM*, no.186 (Baghdad Mus.) – 'Ur III', lapis lazuli; similar but with inscription; the worshipper has his hand at his waist, rather than raised; (also no.193). From Tello.

no.183ff. – standing gods. From Tello.

*OxfordANE* 1, no.420 – Ur III, mottled light and dark green 'steatite'; a similar scene but the standing god now wears a flounced robe, the worshipper raises his right hand and there is an inscription.

Post-Akkadian: 2192–2112 BC

**15**     3:2

**15**  86/1966 (Corkill, S.17)
From Tello(?)

**Cylinder seal**, chlorite, black (and brown). 21 × 11mm

*Presentation (or intercession?) scene*: the main goddess wearing a flounced robe and horned head-dress is seated facing to the right on a chair with a curved back. She has her left hand raised and is approached by two figures who have their right hands raised and left ones at waist level; they wear plain robes – one rather shorter than the other. Above is a crescent moon and below it, in front of the goddess, are parallel zig-zag lines (legs of a child or animal, water?). Terminal, a tree.

It is very unusual for the seated deity to face right but there are a few examples (see below). The goddess's horned head-dress and flounced robe were to become more usual in the Ur III period, but the tree terminal, instead of an inscription, is a Post-Akkadian feature (see also **14**). The seal is rather worn and so it is impossible to determine the details of the hair styles or head-dresses of the other two figures. Parrot (*GM*, pp.46–7) suggests that when the goddess stands behind the worshipper rather than leads him towards the deity, an 'intercession' rather than a 'presentation' scene is intended (cf. **13** – a two figure variation on the intercession scene). It is not clear what the zig-zag lines in front of the deity represent; legs and water are often shown in this way but there is no sign of a body or a vessel. (See *EGAZ*, nos.555–60 for gods with children.)

For scenes with the deity facing to the right, see:

*GM*, nos.136,169–71 – 'Ur III' presentation scenes (no.136, diorite with an inscription) with the main deity facing to the right but with the goddess leading the worshipper by the hand. From Tello.

*LondonWA* 2, nos.413–15 – Ur III, calcite, brown and white jasper and chlorite; the main deity faces to the right; all excavated at Ur (p.146).

*OxfordANE* 1, no.392 – Post-Akkadian, 'steatite'; goddess seated facing right on box-throne with back as on the Exeter seal.

Post-Akkadian: 2192–2112 BC

**16**   (see also frontispiece)                                    3:2

**16**   86/1966 (Corkill, S.7)
From Tello(?)

**Cylinder seal**, chlorite, black (and pale green).
28 × 15mm

*Presentation scene*: a shaven-headed worshipper, with his right hand raised and wearing a fringed robe, is led by a goddess with left hand raised who wears a striped robe with horizontal lines round the hem. They approach a seated goddess in a flounced robe who holds up her right hand. Both goddesses have their robes draped over their right shoulder, wear horned head-dresses and have their hair in a loop behind. Above is a crescent moon and below it, in front of the seated goddess, is a lizard. A libation vessel with a long neck and spout (but no handle), a flying bird(?), a walking bird (a goose?), a scorpion and a fish(?) are framed within two partly erased vertical lines.

This is close to what had become the 'standard' Ur III presentation scene (*London WA* 2, pp.145–6) although it is more usual for goddesses and other figures to have their robes draped over the left shoulder rather than the right. The main goddess usually sits on a box-like throne (often raised on a dais) but here the seal is chipped where the throne should be. (Compare also the earlier Post-Akkadian presentation scenes **13–15**.)

Two or three lines of inscription had become usual at this time but on this seal they appear to have been erased later in the Ur III period and filling motifs added instead; the vertical lines of the frame for an inscription can still be seen. Seals were often re-used and inscriptions erased in this way. Filling motifs – often symbols of particular gods – probably added to the amuletic value of a seal (see *FI*, pp.120–22 for the re-use of seals).

This was the most common type of scene on Ur III cylinder seals and many examples were found at Tello (see *GM*, p.23). Compare:

*GM*, no.104ff. – several are similar in style to the Exeter seal but have inscriptions rather than filling ornaments – e.g. nos.104,124,126 (Louvre AO.15431, AO.16814, Baghdad Mus.) – all from Tello.

*London WA* 2, nos.366–428 – Ur III presentation scenes usually with inscriptions; some with variations and filling ornaments (see pp.145–6 for the 'standard' presentation scene).

no.371 – mottled green serpentine; filling ornaments instead of an inscription.

nos.384–90 – filling ornaments and inscriptions.

no.403 (= *FI*, no.514) – chlorite; a close parallel and the same filling ornaments added over an erased inscription – the line of the frame is still visible. From Ur.

no.466 – agate, mottled reddish and light brown; a similar libation vessel in the field.

Ur III: 2112–2004 BC

**17**

3:2

**17** 86/1966 (Corkill, S.20)
From Tello(?)

**Cylinder seal**, marble, white and brown.
20 × 9mm

*Presentation scene*: a goddess(?) with left hand raised leads a worshipper, his right arm held at waist level, towards a deified king seated on a dais. He wears a turban (or crested cap?) and a long striped or flounced robe, and holds out a cup in his right hand. The worshipper wears a high conical head-dress and the leading goddess a horned head-dress(?); both are in long striped robes. Between the standing figures is a ball-and-staff; in front of the god is a monkey and behind him a pot and a lion-headed scimitar (the symbol of the god Nergal). Above is a crescent moon.

This shows a number of features typical of the earlier part of the Isin/Larsa period (ca.2000–1900 BC) before the rise of the First Dynasty of Babylon. Cylinder seals of this type differ from those of the Ur III period in various ways, for example: the worshipper now often wears a head-dress and no longer raises his left hand; certain filling ornaments become typical – especially the ball-and-staff and pot, as well as the monkey (which often sits in front of deified kings).

This seal, however, can be dated to the early Isin/Larsa period (early 2nd millennium BC) as the goddess still leads the worshipper by the hand as she does on Ur III seals. (On later examples she stands behind the worshipper with both hands raised.) These cylinders are often of poor quality and this seal is also rather worn so that the details of head-dresses and robes are difficult to make out. (For Isin/Larsa seals see *LondonWA* 3, pp.59–61; *FI*, p.44.)

Compare similar early Isin/Larsa presentation scenes:

*LondonWA* 3, nos.1–30 – the goddess still leads the worshipper by the hand; typical filling motifs.
  no.1 (= *FI*, no.153) – goethite; similar but with inscription behind the throne; filling motifs: ball-and-staff and pot.
  nos.2,19 – filling motifs: ball-and-staff and pot, and monkey.
  nos.11–12 – a lion-headed scimitar behind a seated goddess.
*GM*, no.149 (Louvre AO.16910) – Larsa period, grey-green stone; the goddess leads the worshipper; a scimitar behind the deity (but no ball-and-staff and pot). From Tello.
*Yale*, no.706 – 'Steatite'; a suppliant rather than a leading goddess; cursory engraving and worn.
Frankfort, pl.26a (Louvre, As.35/8) – presentation scene to deified king; lion-headed scimitar. Excavated at Tell Asmar.

Early Isin/Larsa: about 2000–1900 BC

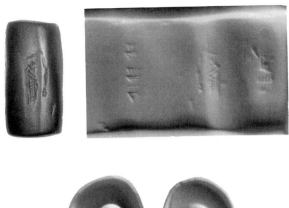

**18**                                                                        3:2

2:1

**18**  86/1966 (Corkill, S.16)
From Tello(?)

**Cylinder seal**, black haematite.
20 × 11–9mm

*Two figures and an inscription* almost entirely erased: a king with mace before a supliant goddess who has both hands raised and wears a flounced robe. The king's right arm can be seen at his side as well as the rolled edges and fringe of his short robe; the top of his mace, which he holds at his waist, is just visible. An incomplete inscription of three cuneiform signs (presumably giving the personal name of the seal owner):

ga? – ša – ni/dù
(or ì/dù)

From the Old Babylonian period in the 2nd millennium BC, quartz (H=6.5–7) and haematite (H=5–6) were commonly used for cylinder seals. These were very hard materials to work and it has been recently suggested that the cutting wheel (often used in conjunction with other methods) was introduced for the first time during this period (see introductory remarks p.2 and cf. the Neo-Babylonian quartz cylinders **23–5**).

Dark materials became popular at this time and haematite was very often used for Old Babylonian seals (see also **20–1**). The engraving has been almost entirely erased; the cylinder is irregular in shape and triangular in section with three flattened sides. When the diameter of a seal is less than half its height (as the smallest diameter is here), the earlier design has probably been erased; the perforation is often re-bored and large (cf.**21**).

The suppliant goddess has been identified with the goddess Lama who, besides protecting the king, acted as an intermediary between a supplicant and a major deity. By about 1800 BC she is often shown with the king with mace. This is a standard scene on Old Babylonian seals and it replaces the presentation scenes of earlier periods (*London WA* 3, pp.100–4; *FI*, Old Babylonian Seals, pp.45–7). For the motif compare **19**.

This is the most common subject at this time and there are many examples:

*London WA* 3, no.161ff. (no.163=*FI*, no.166 – magnetite).
*GM*, no.236 (Baghdad Mus.) – agate; figure in royal posture with goddess. From Tello. (There appear to be few seals of this period from Tello.)

Old Babylonian: 1900–1595 BC

**19**  (see also frontispiece)

3:2

**19**   5/1946.409 (Montague no.265, p.25)

**Cylinder seal**, serpentinite, black (and brown).
(confirmed by XRD analysis)
24 × 9mm

Publ.: *Expert* (Feb.1909) p.63, fig.3

*A King(?) before a suppliant goddess*: a kilted figure
wearing a pointed hat, in royal posture with his
right hand at his side and the other held at waist
level, stands before a suppliant goddess. She raises
both(?) hands and wears a flounced robe and high
head-dress. A four line framed inscription:

| | |
|---|---|
| ᵈnin-kar-nun-na | (Ninkarnunna, |
| an uraš giš-tuku | Who makes |
| | Heaven and |
| | Earth obey |
| | |
| šid-dù é-šu-me-ša₄ | Caretaker of |
| | (the temple) |
| | Eshumesha, |
| | |
| ki-ti sum ìr-na | Who bestows a |
| | protective angel |
| | on his servant.) |

The engraving is rather cursory and linear; the
details are not clear as the seal is very worn –
serpentinite is much softer than haematite. This
is related to the scene on **18** but on this seal it
may not be the king standing before the goddess
Lama as there is no sign of a mace; the hat and
dress of the standing figure are also different
(see *London WA* 3, p.36 for figures of this type).
The figure of the goddess appears to be partly
erased as the surface is flattened; the king might
also have been partly erased but this is less
obvious.

Owners often describe themselves on their seals
as 'servants' and in the Old Babylonian period an
invocation to the deity to bestow a favour on the
worshipper is usual. This inscription seems
unusual. Ninkarnunna was the divine barber (i.e.
vizier) of the god Ninurta whose temple,
Eshumesha, was at Nippur.

Compare:

*London WA* 3, no.203 – haematite; both figures
   wear pointed hats; the goddess raises one
   hand; inscription.
Delaporte 2 (1923) – pl.82, no.22 (A.424) –
   haematite; similar hats; a large space left
   blank.

Old Babylonian: 1900–1595 BC

**20**                                                                                 3:2

**20**   5/1946.408 (Montague no.264, p.25)
Found at Nineveh in 1865

**Cylinder seal**, black haematite.
17–20+ × 13mm (bottom of cylinder broken
off)

Publ.: *Expert* (Feb.1909) p.62, fig.2.

*Two suppliant goddesses* with both hands raised
stand one on either side of a framed three
line inscription; they wear head-dresses and
flounced robes. In front of the goddess on
the left of the inscription is a crook with a
moon and star-disc above; behind the
goddesses is a triple lightning fork and a
double lion-headed mace. The inscription
which follows the usual formula is
incomplete:

| | |
|---|---|
| ka-ag-ga-d[u-(um)] | (Qaqqad[um] |
| DUMU ì-lí-šar?-[rum] | Son of Ili-shar[rum?] |
| ÌR ᵈ[...] | Servant of the god [...]) |

The lower part of the figures and the inscription
are missing as the cylinder is broken. Quartzes
were used most commonly for this group of seals
and haematite is unusual. Astral symbols and
filling motifs seldom appear and a large space is
usually left behind the figures. (For a discussion
see *LondonWA* 3, pp.9–10 (for materials), 199–200,
nos.565–76.)
   From the time of Samsu-iluna (1749–1712 BC) a
pair of goddesses flank the inscription and texts
refer to the 'goddesses Lama'. Deities could be

invoked in three ways on seals: they could be
depicted, their symbol shown or their name
inscribed.
   On this cylinder the crook and star-disc appear
to have been engraved originally as adequate
space has been left for them between the goddess
and the inscription. The more cursorily engraved
lightning fork and double lion-headed mace fill
the space which is usually left blank on this type
of seal; these were probably added later in the
Old Babylonian period.

1. *Star-disc and crescent* – developed in the Ur III
   period, is the symbol of the sun-god Shamash.
2. *Crook* – symbol of the god Amurru (god of the
   Amorites).
3. *Lightning fork* – sometimes held by the weather
   god, Adad.
4. *Double lion-headed mace* – attribute of the warrior
   deities, Ishtar and Nergal.

These symbols appear in various combinations
on other scenes with the suppliant goddess: the
lightning fork and double lion-headed mace are
shown together on *LondonWA* 3, no.222; the
Star-disc and crescent appear above the crook
on nos.505–6 and with the lightning fork on
no.525.

For figures with an inscription, see:

*LondonWA* 3, no.565–76 – mostly quartz (no
   haematite examples).
   no.571 – quartz; a crook between one goddess
   and the inscription.
   no.573 – quartz; a mace in front of one goddess.
Marcopoli, no.126 – haematite, 1750–1700 BC; no
   filling motifs (pp.25–6).

Old Babylonian: about 1800 BC

**21**                                                                              3:2

**21**   5/1946.411 (Montague no.267, p.25)

**Cylinder**, black haematite.
25 × 10–9mm

A *blank cylinder*, unevenly polished with one side flattened and the surface pitted in places.

The perforation, which is off-centre, is large and flared at one end. This may belong to the Old Babylonian period (like **18,20**) when haematite was most popular. Seals were often re-used (see *FI*, pp.120–22; and **18** here).

?Old Babylonian: 1900–1595 BC

**22**                                                                              3:2

**22**   86/1966 (Corkill, S.18)
From Tello(?)

**Cylinder seal**, faience (sintered quartz), probably originally green rather than yellow.
21 × 8mm

A *Procession* of three men and two rampant (horned?) animals walking to the right.

The surface is pitted and details are not visible. The figures have been filled in with purple copying-ink.
    Northern Mesopotamia and Syria had become part of the Mitannian kingdom in the third quarter of the 15th century BC. Faience or sintered quartz, a composition material, appeared towards the mid 2nd millennium BC. Seals in this material were not moulded but were cut, fired and glazed. They could be mass-produced and were widely distributed. The colours were originally bright and they were probably worn as jewellery and amulets.
    There are variations in style and iconography but many of the seals can be attributed to particular workshops. This seal belongs to the 'Mitannian Common style'. Rampant animals and walking figures possibly illustrate a ritual connected with hunting. For a study of Mitannian seals see E. Porada, 'Seal Impressions of Nuzi', *Annual of the American Schools of Oriental Research* 24 (1947); also *FI*, pp.61–5.

For Mitannian seals showing processions of men and rampant animals, see:

Frankfort, pl.43f. – four men and three antelopes walk to the left; from Lachish.

Porada, *op.cit.*, pl.22, nos.441–53 – two or more figures alternating with rampant animals walk in the same direction; Group X (pp.30–3).

Marcopoli, no.577 – ca.1550–1350 BC; two figures with arms raised face two rampant antelopes; (pp.91–2).

Mitannian: 14th century BC

**23** (see also frontispiece)

3:2

**23**    86/1966 (Corkill, S.11)
From Tello(?)

**Cylinder seal**, cornelian (pale red-browns).
23 × 10mm

*A kneeling hero* facing to the right grasps the fore-leg of a horned animal (a goat?) in his left hand and its muzzle in his right hand. The animal is in a contorted position with its head turned back so it appears to face him on the left and turn away from him on the right. In the field above is a star.

This seal is in the Neo-Babylonian cut style of the 9th–7th century BC. The figures have been drawn in a cursory schematic manner with wide grooves of the cutting wheel but without round drill holes or narrow grooves for detailing, which gives the seal an unfinished appearance. (For the use of the cutting wheel which probably appeared for the first time during the Old Babylonian period see introductory remarks p.2; cf. also **24–5**.)
This type of composition is first attested on

Middle Assyrian cylinders of the 14th century BC where one animal and a tree, or a contest scene with two contestants, appear as a continuous frieze (*FI*, pp.66–7, nos.277,279 and examples below). In impression the Exeter seal can appear as a continuous frieze or can give the illusion of either a hero between two animals or an animal between two heroes.

Though there is some overlapping of styles and subject matter in Neo-Assyrian and Neo-Babylonian seals, it has been possible to distinguish certain features which are more typical of one group than the other *FI*, p.75ff.; *Orientalia* 16, p.145ff.

Cut style seals were produced in both Assyria and Babylonia in the 8th–7th century BC.

For the same type of composition and cut style seals, see:

*Corpus*, no.595 (=*FI*, no.279) – 14th or 13th century BC, Middle Assyrian chalcedony; a griffin grasping the tail and muzzle of a bull; an earlier example of this composition.

*OxfordANE* 1, no.652 – Neo-Babylonian late 8th–7th century BC, limestone; cut style but influenced by the modelled style; the same motif as on the Exeter seal but the kneeling hero does not actually grasp the goat; some filling objects.

nos.645–59 – cut style seals, p.116.

*BerlinVARS*, pl.75, nos.626,631, esp.nos.633,635 – very similar cut style to the Exeter seal without round drill holes or narrow grooves for detailing.

*Orientalia* 16, pl.8, fig.29 – later cut style of

8th–7th century; similar technique to the Exeter seal; the changing depth of incisions gives an illusion of modelling typical of the glyptic art of Assyria and Babylonia at this time.

Neo-Babylonian Cut style: about 9th–7th century BC

**24**   (see also frontispiece)                                                                                                   3:2

**24**   5/1946.412 (Montague no.267a, p.25)
Acquired from Major Moore 29/12/18
(see p.132)

**Cylinder seal**, chalcedony (pale grey-brown).

33 × 14mm

*Contest scene*: a winged genie with a sickle sword, held in one hand behind him, steps forward to grasp the front leg of a rampant, winged human-headed bull wearing a conical hat; both have long hair and a beard. The genie wears a long striped or flounced mantle with a fringed hem, open down the front to reveal a kilt and his leg as he places his left foot on a recumbent gazelle turning its head back. In the field are two smaller standing gazelles looking backwards, a cactus plant and several small drill holes; above is a standard (the object on the top is worn off), a star and a crescent.

A fine quality seal engraved with a cutting wheel and drill in the Neo-Babylonian modelled style. The figures have an effect of plasticity, and details of textiles, wings and hair are drawn with very fine shallow lines.

No close chronology has been established yet for Neo-Assyrian and Neo-Babylonian cylinders because of a lack of dated comparative archaeological material. The two groups overlap in style and iconography but there are some differences (see *FI*, pp.75–83). There is, however, a specifically Neo-Babylonian group of cylinders in a modelled style which can be identified by certain characteristics (see E. Porada in *Orientalia* 16, p.145ff.; *Corpus*, pp.90–1). The composition on this seal is based on a Middle Assyrian type but a number of Neo-Babylonian characteristics are evident here:

1. The pose of the genie confronting a single opponent with his weapon held pointing down behind him and stepping on the back of the victim. (On Neo-Assyrian seals two opponents, one on either side of the hero, are more usual.)

2. The upper and lower wings of equal size are also typically Neo-Babylonian.

3. The cactus plant often appears on Neo-Babylonian seals but rarely on Neo-Assyrian seals.

4. The genie and the human-headed bull's large outlined eyes.

Related Neo-Babylonian cylinder seals appear in:

*Orientalia* 16, pl.3, fig.3 – modelled style 10th–8th century BC; a close parallel though the opponent is a sphinx and the genie wears a short kilt and high feathered crown; in the field a star, crescent and standards.

Fig.7 – a cactus in the field.

Fig.8 – genie in similar long flounced garment and head-dress.

Fig.9 – cornelian; as above but only one pair of wings is shown; (he wears a horned diadem).

*FI*, no.366ff. – similar scenes in the Neo-Babylonian modelled style.

Neo-Babylonian: 8th–7th century BC

**25**                                                                                     3:2

**25**   5/1946.410 (Montague, no.266)
Excavated at Nineveh

**Cylinder seal**, pink chalcedony.
23 × 10mm

Publ.: *Expert* (Feb.1909) p.63, fig.4.

*Contest scene*: a four-winged genie with a long beard grasps a sphinx on the left by the tail as it tries to escape, and a rampant sphinx on the right by its fore-paw; they all have their head turned to the right. The genie wears a cap(?) and a kilt with a pattern of squares and dots. The winged sphinxes have lions' bodies with a fringe of fur under the abdomen and female(?) heads; they wear conical ridged turbans.

This is another fine quality seal in the Neo-Babylonian modelled style engraved with the cutting wheel and drill. Details are carefully shown and the modelling is deeper than on **23** with more emphasis on muscles and anatomy.

The four wings of the genie which are of equal size (on Assyrian seals the lower ones are often longer) and the contorted posture of the sphinx on the left with its head turned back are also typically Neo-Babylonian. (The hero with two opponents is more typically Neo-Assyrian but the compositions are usually more symmetrical.) This type of textile with a pattern of squares had been introduced by the middle of the 8th century BC under western influence. Sphinxes are most common in the 1st millennium BC though they first occur in Akkadian times. Porada points out that late contest scenes show a return to Akkadian types where the hero grapples with two opponents with his bare hands.

For Neo-Babylonian and Assyrian modelled style cylinders see *Corpus*, pp.91–2; *FI*, pp.80–3.

For similar seals of the Neo-Babylonian period see:

*FI*, no.371 (BM 100674) – two genii in kilts with patterns of squares and dots, and a sphinx in contorted posture below.

no.372 (*BerlinVARS*, no.735) – a genie wearing a similarly patterned kilt with two lions; very close in style to the Exeter seal. From Babylon.

no.964 (BM 130807) – Neo-Assyrian pink chalcedony; very similar in style though the hero, who grapples with a rampant sphinx and bull, wears a long robe.

*Corpus*, no.758 – olive-buff chert 'Neo-Babylonian and Assyrian modelled style late contest scene'; a winged hero in long robe grapples with two rampant female sphinxes; the modelled style of the engraving and especially the sphinxes are very similar to the Exeter seal.

Neo-Babylonian: late 8th century BC

**26**                                                                                                    3:2

**26**   86/1966 (Corkill, S.10)
From Tello(?)

**Cylinder seal**, chalcedony (pale brownish-grey).
22–23 × 11mm (very narrow perforation, less than 2mm)

*A Horseman* (with head missing) rides to the left chasing a prancing gazelle (or antelope?) which turns its head back towards him. The reins appear to hang loose and the rider has one hand between the horse's ears and the other on its rump. There are trappings round the horse's neck and hanging down beneath its belly.

This cylinder seal is in the 7th century BC Neo-Elamite style which is characterized by animals in

lively attitudes with arched necks. Hunting scenes were to influence later Achaemenid iconography; in this case the rider does not carry a weapon. The rider's pose with one hand on the animal's rump is reminiscent of one on an earlier seal where the unsteady rider grips the mane and tail of his horse (*FI*, no.737 (Louvre AO 7223) – Old Babylonian period).

For similar seals of this period see:

*FI*, no.411 (BM 103013) – 7thc. BC Neo-Elamite, limestone; a hunter and animal in similar attitude (pp.86–9).

*Corpus*, no.812 – proto-Achaemenian/Elamite chalcedony; a hunter spearing an antelope; very similar to the Exeter seal.

Marcopoli, no.288 – Achaemenid, ca.650–521 BC, agate; kneeling archer and mouflon; similar style.

Neo-Elamite: 7th century BC

**27**  5/1946.379 (Montague no.236f, p.21A)
From Clements (7s 6d) 1917 (see p.131)

**Oval conoid stamp seal**, chalcedony;
perforated; chipped.
ht.27 × w.16/20mm (perforation: diam.
ca.4mm)
Intaglio face: 18 × 15mm convex

**27**                                   4:1

A *Bearded worshipper* with hands raised and
wearing a long garment stands in profile
facing to the right between divine emblems:
in front of him a plant(?) and behind him a
cross-shaped standard. Groundline.

The worshipper with emblems is the most
common subject on Neo-Babylonian stamp seals
from the late 7th–6th century BC. (Versions are
also found on contemporary cylinder seals and
the theme continues into the Achaemenid
period.) Many of the seals in this group are
engraved in similar stylized fashion. Here the
simplified figure is cut with a broad wheel
groove; his head, hair and shoulder are marked
by round globules; his beard, arms and folds of
his garment are engraved with straight narrow
wheel grooves.

The worshipper is more often shown standing
to the side of the field with the various emblems
(sometimes on an altar) in front of him. Neo-
Babylonian stamp seals of this type are discussed
in *OxfordANE* 3, pp.56–7; and for worshippers in
the Neo-Babylonian and Achaemenid 'drilled'
and 'cut' styles see no.380ff., p.60.

Compare:

*OxfordANE* 3, no.391 – chalcedony; worshipper
    with cross-shaped symbol; engraved in similar
    style.
  nos.396–7 – chalcedony; worshippers before
    plants.
L. Jakob-Rost, *Die Stempelsiegel im Vorderasiatischen
    Museum* (Berlin: 1975), no.258 – chalcedony; a
    worshipper with the cross-standard behind him
    (as on the Exeter gem) faces an altar with other
    emblems in front of him.
D. Collon, *Near Eastern Seals* (1990) no.1D (& cover
    illus.) – 6thc. BC blue chalcedony conoid; a
    rather less stylized example.

Neo-Babylonian: 7th century BC

**28**    5/1946.363 (Montague no.226, p.21)

**Tabloid stamp seal**, bronze; the remains of a bronze wire loop handle fixed into a hole on the right edge; a corresponding hole on the left edge.
15 × 11 × 3mm

A *Goat* with humanoid head walks in profile to the right; it has a large outlined eye seen as if from the front and a beard marked by a double line of globules. A rectangular border of straight lines.

**28**  (see also frontispiece)                    4:1

The animal is finely detailed; its ribs are shown as three grooves, its shoulder is outlined, and there are markings on its haunches – a typically Achaemenid feature. A line of small ridges runs along its spine. There seems to be a flaw in the area where the horns should be which at first glance makes it look as if the goat is wearing a head-dress or hat. (The head might even appear to be a combination humanoid/animal head –

although this would be unusual: the double line of globules would mark the man's beard and substitute for the backward-facing animal's horn (for the substitution of parts, rather than the combination by addition, see *AGGems*, p.84; and compare the angle of the goat's horn on a mid 5th century BC Greek gem, *Intaglios and Rings*, no.42).)

A study of the seal, entitled *Analysis and Metallography of a Stamp Seal*, #R1171, undertaken by Dr J.P. Northover (Department of Materials, University of Oxford), shows that the intaglio was struck rather than cast. (Overlapping cuts, however, suggest that the rectangular frame round the motif was chiselled out after the striking.) The composition of the metal is typical of much ancient Near Eastern bronze of the Achaemenid period: the tin content was estimated as 10–12%, the lead content as less than 1%; and the most significant impurities were iron and arsenic. Examination of the microstructure shows that the bronze for the seal was prepared by cold hammering and annealing a cast block at high temperature. This process would soften and toughen the bronze before cold striking with a die to make the impression, and also facilitate the chisel-cutting of the frame lines afterwards. The die would have been made out of hardened bronze or iron with the motif either carved in relief, or struck from a master die engraved in intaglio. The die face outside the design was large enough and flat enough to leave no marks on the surface of the seal. The flaws and defects on the seal, especially in the area of the horns and the back leg, show that the die was worn, chipped and clogged up in places. The surface of the seal has been deeply penetrated by intergranular corrosion which also obscures some of the detail.

The animal (**28**) closely resembles the walking goat on the bronze tabloid in the M. Shubin collection (**28x**) which is said to have come from near Lake Tiberias in Israel and to be the same as the example in *Malter 58* (1994) no.104. Although there are some differences in the angles of the legs and in the head, the seals (**28** and **28x**) appear to have been made from the same original which may have been altered or touched up at some stage. The head on **28x** appears more goat-like than the head on the Exeter seal (**28**) and the horns growing from its forehead are more obvious – but its body is the same length and there are many similarities in detail. Unfortunately, the line of the frame on **28x** runs along the top of the goat's head, cutting it off where the horns would probably have been which makes it impossible to compare the flawed area (or identify the indistinct object) on **28**. It seems likely that this damaged area had been removed from the die by the time **28x** was struck.

Greek, Achaemenid and local). Seals of this type appear to have come from the Lebanon, Israel and elsewhere in the Middle East, but no examples have so far been recorded from controlled excavations. A number of these seals are in the British Museum and will be published by Dr John Curtis.

For other bronze tabloids with Persian Achaemenid iconography belonging to this group see:

*Malter 58* (1994) no.103 (=**28y**) – two archers in Persian dress drawn in a linear local style (cf. examples in the British Museum for the motif, but not the style.)
   no.104 (=**28z**) – a roaring lion passant, in Achaemenid style (cf. BM 1991–10–5, 2 & 10); and a goat passant (not illustrated) but said to be the same as **28x** here.

**28x**                                    4:1

                                          2:1

*(M. Shubin collection)*

**28y**

**28z**                                   2:1

*(Courtesy of Malter Galleries & A.L. Wolfe)*

*The bronze tabloid group*: both these seals (**28** and **28x**) belong to a recently identified group of square or rectangular bronze tabloid seals with iconography from various traditions (including

These bronze tabloid seals are not perforated right through (like steatite tabloids) but have holes in two edges for inserting a bronze wire handle which is pinched in close to the back and expands to form a loop. The handle on these seals is often missing or partly broken off but it is still complete on **28x** and on BM 1991–10–5,5 – a Persian horseman (cf. also the gold wire handle on the 8th–7th century BC Syrian scaraboid, *Intaglios and Rings*, no.209). Some of the seals have no border round the motif (**28y**), others (perhaps influenced by scarabs or cubicals) have a hatched, globular or plain linear border like the Exeter seal. It is possible that these bronze seals had some special administrative function.

Although the shape and form of this group of bronze seals is more or less the same, their iconography is eclectic and the quality of engraving is variable – often linear and stylized. The seals with recognizably Persian Achaemenid iconography are usually less cursorily engraved and more carefully detailed than the others; they can be dated 5th–4th century BC. Although both goat seals, **28** and **28x**, have Achaemenid features, the iconography is unusual and there is no exact parallel. Examples in the British Museum illustrate Persian horsemen, walking Persian bowmen and kneeling Greek warriors with plumed helmets (one example has Persians in the upper register and Greeks in the lower). Two others have single walking lions very similar to those on the glazed brick reliefs at Susa. Their muscles are shown as a complex, stylized pattern – comparable to the stylization on the Exeter seal and the lion, **28z** (see above).

A silver ring excavated in the Lebanon appears to be closely related to the bronze tabloid group and is securely dated 5th–4th century BC:

*Kāmid el-Lōz* (1996) pp.121–2, no.67 – silver ring with a rectangular bezel supported on volutes at the ends of the hoop (from grave no.7). The scene is divided into two fields: in the lower field four figures move in procession or dance to the right; and above are two seven-pointed stars. A cable pattern border of hatched lines frames the whole scene and divides the two fields. (A close parallel from 'Atlīt is cited.) The iconography appears related to the post-Assyrian/Levantine tradition and is similar to the three-figure procession on a bronze tabloid in the British Museum (BM 1991–10–5,6).

*The Tabloid shape*: the tabloid shape appears to have had a long history in the Ancient Near East going back to prehistoric times but it is not found in Iran itself in the first millennium BC. However, Greco-Persian tabloids decorated on one or more surfaces occur in the western Persian empire (e.g. *GGFR*, nos.976–7). Various other types of tabloid, often in black steatite, have been found in Cyprus and the Syro-Phoenician region of the mainland. There appears to be some connection between these tabloids, the bronze seals and a group of steatite cubical seals from Cyprus (see the discussion of tabloids and cubicals below).

*Mixed styles and iconography*: the mixing of cultural traditions seems to have occurred early (see for example the two-sided steatite tabloid from a Late Bronze Age grave, ca.1175 BC, *Kāmid el-Lōz* (1996) no.49 – Egyptianizing on one side, Levantine on the other). In the Achaemenid empire the interaction of many cultural traditions and influences led to mixed styles and iconography on seals of various shapes (see *OxfordANE* 3, 'Stamp Seals of the Achaemenid Empire', p.68ff.). The impact of Achaemenid iconography on local and other styles is well illustrated on a large steatite tabloid of Near Eastern type engraved on four sides (*OxfordANE* 3, no.453, and P.R.S. Moorey, 'The Iconography of an Achaemenid Stamp-Seal acquired in the Lebanon', *Iran* 16 (1978) pp.143–54, pl.1a).

Related phenomena are illustrated by several groups of seals in the Eastern Mediterranean area and the Middle East but the 'mixing' can take place in various ways giving very different results. These bronze tabloids probably come from quite a limited geographical area and show how a particular shape of seal (probably local) can persist but become the vehicles for different iconographical traditions.

This phenomenon is well illustrated in E. Gubel, ''Syro-Cypriote' Cubical Stamps: the Phoenician connection', *Studia Phoenicia* V (1987) pp.195–224, where a group of culturally eclectic cubical steatite seals engraved on five surfaces are discussed. The cubical shape persisted for several centuries from about the 9th century BC but the engraving shows a mixture of different iconographic and stylistic influences (often on the same seal) – Phoenician, Syrian, Greek, and Cypriot. Two cubical seals are dated to the 6th century BC: the first (fig.1) belongs to the Cypro-Archaic II period and shows a combination of Greek and Cypro-Oriental elements, while the second shows Greek features and was found in a burial with an Achaemenid bracelet (see V.

Karageorghis, 'Chronique des fouilles et découvertes archéologiques à Chypre en 1969', *BCH* 94 (1970) pp.207–8, fig.34).

It has been pointed out that steatite tabloid seals are related to cubical seals (see W. Culican, 'Syrian and Cypriot Cubical Seals', *Levant* 9 (1977) p.162ff., esp. p.166). Like the cubicals they show mixed styles and iconography and also sometimes have linear or double linear borders with hatching in between, like a number of the bronze seals. Two steatite tabloids from Cyprus, dated to the 7th century BC, have been compared to the ca.7th century BC 'Pyrga' group of cubicals: see *Berlin*, nos.125–6 (cf. also *OxfordANE* 3, no.530 – although this is dated much earlier). Some of the more stylized scenes on this 'Pyrga' group also resemble, both in style and iconography, motifs on some of the bronze tabloids in the British Museum. This establishes a link between all three groups: the steatite tabloids and cubicals, and the bronze tabloids. As with the 6th century BC cubical seals, the bronze tabloids in Persian or Greco-Persian style might be slightly later in date than the linear and stylized examples which reflect other traditions. Although it is now accepted that the Cypriot kingdoms became part of the Persian Empire around 525 BC, few gems in the Achaemenid Court Style are said to have been found in Cyprus (see A.T. Reyes, 'Cyprus and Persia', *Archaic Cyprus* (1994) pp.85,97).

In Palestine during the Persian period there seems to have been a similar phenomenon though tabloid seals and tabloid seal impressions seem unusual (see E. Stern, in *Material Culture from the Land of the Bible in the Persian Period* (1982) p.196ff., esp. pp.199–200). Local seals of mixed style were produced (sometimes probably by Phoenicians) which in form or motifs imitate Babylonian, Egyptian, Greek and also Achaemenid imports. These seals (like the Cypriot examples) often combined the iconography from one tradition with the seal-shape of another. Large caches of bullae have been found which show that many types and styles of seal were used in the same administrative office; but there is only one rectangular impression (pp.208–9).

A shallow Achaemenid ceramic tray (6th–4th century BC) with a small semi-circular depression opposite the handle and which stands on curved loop-like feet has seven rectangular seal impressions on the underside made from two seals: one shows a walking warrior with bowcase and upright spear, and the other a winged walking animal. The outlines and edges of the impressions appear sharp which may suggest that they were made with metal seals and the motifs are similar to some of those on the bronze tabloid group described here. The impressions, however, are much larger, ca.50 × 30mm, (see T.S. Kawami, *Ancient Iranian Ceramics from the Arthur M. Sackler Collections* (1992) p.221, no.130 = S.1987.947). The purpose of the repetitive impressions seems unclear but could be purely decorative.

*The iconography of the Exeter seal*: although the Exeter tabloid shows provincial influence from the western part of the empire, it is closely related to the Achaemenid Court Style. Walking animals, monsters (often winged) with bearded human heads or mixed monsters are popular on Persian stamp seals from the western empire, but walking goats with humanoid heads seem unusual. The coarse facial features, though, resemble those on goat-sphinxes (see J. Boardman, 'Pyramidal Stamp Seals in the Persian Empire', *Iran* 8 (1970) p.34, especially no.137, and for the Achaemenid Court Style and the fusion of Greek and Persian styles and motifs p.32ff.; for other monsters see *GGFR*, pls.825, 837ff., and the Court Style, pp.305–9). The head is also reminiscent of the humanoid ram-head on an Archaic statuette of the Phoenician god Baal-Hamman, 600–500 BC, whose cult was found on Cyprus and the Syro-Phoenician mainland as well as in Carthage (see V. Karageorghis, *Two Cypriote Sanctuaries of the end of the Cypro-Archaic Period* (1977) pp.35–6, no.1, pls.6, 29 (=*Cyprus, 7000 Years of History* (BM Catalogue, 1979) pp.95–6, no.291).

The stylized body markings with patterns of globules can be compared to the 6th–5th century BC animal reliefs and bull capitals from the Palace of Darius at Susa and Persepolis (e.g. R. Ghirshman, *Persia from the Origins to Alexander the Great* (1984) pls.191–2 – a lion griffin and a winged bull on glazed brick reliefs (Susa); pl.240 – relief of a lion attacking a bull, and pl.261 – a bull capital (Persepolis)). The horned animals (or ibex) on an Achaemenid style 5th century BC gold earring also show similar stylization (see W. Culican, *The Medes and the Persians*, no.67 = Ghirshman, *op.cit.* pl.323).

Achaemenid Provincial: 5th–4th century BC

**29**  5/1946.354 (Montague no.217, p.20)
From Tripoli, Syria (see p.133)

**Pyramidal pendant**, brownish chalcedony; irregular and chipped; intagli on the two larger sides, (i) & (ii), and a perforation at the apex.
ht.28 × base ca.19 × 12mm

Publ.: *Bazaar*, 9/7/13, pp.53–4, fig.13

(i) *A Man stands facing to the right with his left arm raised*: a cloak is draped over his right shoulder and falls over his bent right arm.

(ii) *A Man stands on one leg* (in a dancing or perhaps seated position); he rests his elbow on the other leg which is raised and bent at the knee.

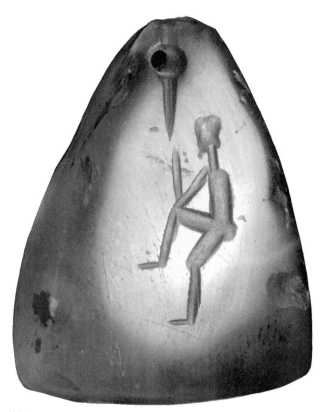

**(ii)**  (see also frontispiece)                                    4:1

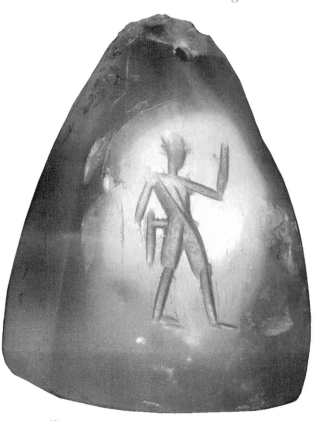

**29 (i)**

Montague writes that 'This remarkable amulet is evidently very ancient, but neither Egyptian, Greek, nor Roman and differing from any Babylonian and Sassanian engraved stones as illustrated by King, though more like these in style than any other class with which I am acquainted. I am inclined to think it may be Carthaginian.' (*Bazaar*, *loc.cit.*). This pendant (which can be also used as a seal) was among the amulets which had been acquired in Tripoli, Syria (see p.133 & **87–93**).

The shape of this pendant is unusual but is perhaps in the tradition of the pear-shaped pendants in the Mixed Greco-Persian style from the western Persian empire which have single figures engraved on the sides (*GGFR*, pl.891, fig.294, pp.312–13, 316–17). Alternatively, it may be a Babylonian or Assyrian stone (perhaps originally intended for a stamp seal cf. **27**) which has been re-cut and had the two engraved figures added later. The suspension hole is very near the apex and pierces a vertical groove on one side.

The stick-like figures seem unfinished and roughly sketched in with straight wheel grooves without detailing. They appear to be in essentially classical poses. The standing figure (i) (with 'arm raised in attitude of worship') has a cloak draped round him rather like Mercury (cf. **37,56–7**). The other figure (ii) with only one arm visible, possibly has his foot raised as if it were to have rested on an object which was never engraved (although he does lean back rather far and would have been off-balance); compare the warrior-types with foot resting on the prow of a ship or on a pile of stones which are possibly derived from a 4th century BC statue by Lysippus (*GGFR*, pls.535,537, p.201 – end 5th to the beginning of the 4thc. BC; and Roman examples, *Dalmatian Gems* nos.162–5 and esp.no.166). Alternatively he could be in a seated or dancing position (cf. *Munich* i, no.373 – a 3rdc. BC Hellenistic gem showing a cult dancer).

The engraving is most probably unfinished, but otherwise the style resembles a few gems in the Bern group which are post-Achaemenid in date. Here too there is little detail in the figures and almost no use of the round drill – see *GGFR*, pp.321–2 and especially the chalcedony scaraboid, pl.972 (Paris, BN 1096), where the figure of the Persian spearing the boar is very similar to those on the pendant (cf. especially the head of pl.972 with figure on side (ii)).

Post Achaemenid: about 3rd century BC or later?

## II  GREEK AND ROMAN GEMS AND RINGS: (30–65)

In Iron Age Greece new sources of inspiration from the East created renewed seal usage in Greek lands. By the Classical period seal engraving had become highly developed in line with the other major achievements of Classical Greek art. It then became usual to mount engraved gems (often scarabs) in swivel rings, incise the bezels of metal rings and mount engraved gems in rings or other objects.

The subjects and styles of seals were transformed by the Greeks, who introduced a larger and more varied repertoire which continued into the Roman period: besides depicting gods, there were heroes, scenes from mythology and daily life, animals, monsters, objects and symbols. Motifs often shed light on contemporary life, religion and works of art.

In the period of the Roman Republic (5th–mid 1st century BC) only certain individuals, notably men of equestrian status and presumably those of higher (senatorial) rank, were entitled to wear gold rings; most rings were made of iron. By the time of the Roman Empire in the 1st century AD, the use of seals had become more widespread and the wearing of gold rings seems to have spread in spite of the sumptuary legislation. In AD 197 under Severus all soldiers became entitled to wear the gold ring, and eventually this privilege was extended to people of lower rank and humble origin.[14] None of the engraved gems in the Exeter collection is set in its original ancient gold ring but a few are still in their iron, bronze, silver or gilt metal settings (e.g. **43,46–9**).

In this collection there are two Greek gems: a glass scaraboid of the 4th century BC Classical period which shows Hercules holding a locust (**30**); and a massive Hellenistic iron ring of the 3rd–2nd century BC (**31**). A few gems – notably the two 'Greco-Roman' gems in Hellenistic style – date to the later Roman Republic, probably the 1st century BC: the very fine bust of a bearded god (**32**) and the cameo head of Serapis (**33**). The majority of gems in this section, however, belong to the Roman Imperial period (about the late 1st century BC–3rd century AD) and, although the collection is by no means comprehensive, it does give some idea of the variety of styles and subject matter usual on engraved gems at this time.

Later Greek and Roman gems were usually made to be set into rings. They were used to validate signatures on contracts and letters or to secure boxes or packages containing valuables, stores or other possessions (cf. Roman Lead Sealings, pp.78–82). The motif on an intaglio was frequently engraved in reverse on the stone, showing it was meant to be viewed in relief, as it appears on the impression (sealing). Cameos (which date from Hellenistic times onwards but belong mainly to the Roman period), on the other hand, are carved in relief. They were not used for sealing and their purpose was mainly decorative and/or amuletic (**33 & 52**). Intagli and cameos sometimes had a purely decorative function and were set into vessels, furniture, or sewn on to clothes.

The device engraved on a gem would be chosen by the owner for whom it probably had a special significance; it could reflect his occupation, aspirations, or beliefs – as well as fears and superstitions. Some gems were used as amulets and have apotropaic qualities; this meant that either the motif, and/or a particular type of stone, was believed to protect the wearer from misfortune, have curative properties, or ward off the evil eye (note especially **47,51–2**, the gnostic gems **53–4** and the amulets, **87ff.**).

The size and shape of gems and their ring settings changed according to fashion. This, as well as the style of engraving, and the motif (especially in the case of portraits) helps with dating – though this must in most cases be only approximate. Gems of different style and quality were, of course, produced concurrently, though from the 2nd century AD there is a general decline in quality. The most common stones used in the Roman period are varieties of quartz: cornelian, chalcedony, jaspers, nicolos, layered agates and amethyst. Glass, which was very often substituted for stone during Julius Caesar's ascendancy (49–44 BC), became very popular from the Augustan era (31 BC–AD 14) onwards. (For materials see Appendix Ia and Ib, pp.135–6.)

Seven other Roman gems and rings in the Museum (which are not part of the Montague or Corkill bequests but are archaeological finds from Devon) have been included at the end of this section (**55–61**); four were found in Exeter, two in the fort at Tiverton and one comes from Seaton Roman villa. They have already been published by Dr Martin Henig who assigns three of them to his distinctive Flavian group (about AD 70–120).

For Greek glyptics see J. Boardman, *Greek Gems and Finger Rings: Early Bronze Age to Late Classical* (1974) (abbr. *GGFR*). For the Greek and later periods see G.M.A. Richter, *Engraved Gems of the Greeks and the Etruscans* (1968), and *Engraved Gems of the Romans* (1971) (abbr. Richter 1 & 2), M. Henig, *Classical Gems: Ancient and Modern Intaglios and Cameos in the Fitzwilliam Museum, Cambridge* (1994) (abbr. *Cambridge*). For stylistic groups and dating of intagli, see M. Maaskant-Kleibrink, *Catalogue of the Engraved Gems in the Royal Coin Cabinet, the Hague: the Greek, Roman and Etruscan Collections* (1978) (abbr. *Hague*). For intagli in Britain see M. Henig, *Corpus of Engraved Gemstones from British Sites*, *BAR* 8 (2nd ed. 1978) (abbr. *Britain*).

## NOTE

14. For a detailed account see M. Deloche, *Le Port des anneaux dans l'antiquité romaine* (1896); also *London Rings*, pp.xviii–xxi.

**30**   5/1946.360 (Montague no.223, p.20 cont.)
Ex coll. Prof. Churchill Babington (see p.131)

**Scaraboid**, glass, greenish yellow, perforated longitudinally; some iridescent patches; the surface pitted and chipped and a large chip off the left side of the gem.
28 × ca.23 × 21mm flat face, convex back.

Publ.: *Bazaar*, 26/6/09, p.1628, fig.9

*Herakles/Hercules*, nude, beardless and with short curly hair, stands with his head in profile and his body turned towards the left in three quarter view; his left leg is flexed with the heel off the ground and his weight is on his right leg; with his left hand against his hip, he holds the top of his downturned club at an angle to his body; in his right hand he holds a locust, grasshopper or cricket (*akris*).

3:1

**30** (see also frontispiece)                    3:1

In the Greek Classical period of the 5th and 4th centuries BC, although scarabs were still being produced, scaraboids became the most popular shape for gems. These were usually perforated longitudinally and were worn as swivel rings, as pendants or on the finger and could be engraved on the flat or the convex side (Richter 1, p.75; *GGFR*, pp.191–2).

Glass scaraboids like the Exeter example were produced as cheap substitutes for gems of semi-precious stones and were cast in one piece in open moulds. Some moulds were made from original engraved gems, and so the glass scaraboid copies would probably just have been touched up after casting; others were cast as blanks and had to have new motifs engraved after casting. Unlike stone scaraboids, glass scaraboids do not have highly domed backs as the molten glass would have levelled off in the mould. They are mostly in clear, pale green or yellow glass. A number of large glass scaraboids of this type have been found in Greece, the Near East, Egypt and Olbia, South Russia (see *GGFR*, pls.642–55 – 5th and 4thc. BC, pp.210–11,415–16; *Intaglios and Rings*, nos.52–3; *Getty*, nos.22–8). The Exeter scaraboid can be dated to the 4th century BC. (Montague wrongly believed the gem was Roman and dated it to the 3rd century AD. He suggested it was an amulet against the 'evil eye' as the Romans considered the *gryllus* or cricket to be apotropaic (*Bazaar, loc.cit.*).)

Herakles' anatomy is carefully detailed with emphasis on the muscles of the torso. His body is accurately foreshortened and he stands in Polykleitan fashion with his weight on one leg and the other bent with his heel off the ground.

This Herakles is derived from a statuary prototype of the 5th century BC. He is often shown in similar fashion on statues, reliefs and coins but in slightly different positions and with a variety of attributes. It has been suggested that the statuary type, usually with a lionskin, may have been adopted in South Italy; it is found on a *didrachm* of Herkaleia, ca.281–272 BC – for a discussion see P.W. Lehmann, *Statues on Coins* (1946) pp.7–8, pl.1, fig.5; *LIMC* iv, no.344. Related types continued to be popular on Italic and Roman gems.

A close parallel showing Herakles standing in the same position (though he is accompanied by Athena) appears on a 4th century BC relief in Athens (*LIMC* iv, Herakles, no.328 – Epigr. Mus.2810). The locust (*akris*) is an unusual attribute for Herakles and this seems to be the only known example of the motif. It recalls a relief by Alxenor, the Naxian, which shows a young man feeding a locust to his dog (J. Boardman, *Greek Sculpture: the Archaic Period* (1978) fig.248, ca.490 BC).

It is uncertain, though, what sort of insect the artist actually intended here. In antiquity there was considerable confusion between the *akris* or locust and *cicada/tettix* group. Although their appearance is quite different both are singing insects. In poetry they were closely associated and the characteristics of one were often transferred to the other. There were many different names for them and it is not always clear which insect is described.

There are two traditions which associate Herakles with locusts and cicadas and it is likely that there is an allusion to one of them here:

Herakles was supposed to have had the power to ward off destructive plagues of locusts which were sometimes regarded as a sign of divine displeasure.

According to Strabo (13.613.64), he was said to have rid Mt. Oeta of locusts and was worshipped as 'Kornopion' ('kornops' – the word in local dialect for 'parnops' = locust). It is possible that he was syncretized with a local deity. (Pausanias (1.24.8) mentions a statue of Apollo 'Parnopios' on the Acropolis which commemorated the occasion when the god drove away a swarm of locusts in Attica.)

According to Diodorus (4.22.5), Herakles was supposed to have been annoyed by the noise of cicadas when he lay down to rest between the neighbouring regions of Rhegium and Locri in Italy on his return after his fight with Geryones. He dispersed them by prayer and it was said that the cicadas in Rhegium never sang again while those in Locri continued to sing normally.

For Orthoptera (*Akris/locusta* – grasshopper/locust/cricket) and the Hemiptera (*Tettix/Cicada*) see: *Greek Insects*, pp.113–33, 134–48, & Herakles, p.141; I.C. Beavis, *Insects and other Invertebrates in Antiquity*, pp.62–78, 91–103, & Herakles pp.75,98; also *LIMC* v, Herakles, p.120).

For a study of this statuary type with variations on some well-known Greek gems (but none with the locust), see G. Horster, *Statuen auf Gemmen* (1970) pp.16–17, pls.3–4:

*F.Berlin*, no.291 (=*AG*, pl.10.42; Lippold, pl.37.13; Richter 1, no.221; Horster, *op.cit.*, pl.4.1; *LIMC* iv, Herakles, no.771) – late 5th–early 4thc. BC gold ring; 'Herakles bibax' also without a lionskin; a close parallel apart from the cup in his right hand, and a slightly less bent right leg.

*AG*, pl.61.31 (=Horster, *op.cit.*, pl.4.2) – 4thc. BC silver ring; here he wears the lionskin over his head and has a cloak over his arm.

*Berlin*, no.156 (= *F.Berlin*, no.317; *AG*, pl.10.41; Horster, *op.cit.*, pl.4.3) – second quarter of the 4thc. BC rock crystal scaraboid; Herakles holds a bow and has his lionskin over his arm, but his knee is bent in as on the Exeter scaraboid.

*LondonRings*, no.57 (=Horster, *op.cit.*, pl.3.4.) – 4thc. BC gold ring; Herakles in similar pose with Nike holding out a wreath (cf. the relief with Athena in Athens, *LIMC* iv, Herakles, no.328).

Greek, 4th century BC

**31**   5/1946.396 (Montague no.252, p.24)
Ex coll. Prince Hugo Erba Odescalchi (12s
6d) (see p.132)
'Probably found in Italy'

**Intaglio, iron ring**, corroded and rusty;
ovoid flat bezel.
33 × 26 × 4mm
Ring: ht.23 × w.33mm; plano-convex hoop
w.9–19mm
(Ring type as *GGFR*, p.213, Type XVII)

Publ.: *Bazaar*, 6/9/12, pp.482–3, fig.1

*Bust of a man*, possibly bearded, in profile to
the right wearing a flat cap (or *kausia*) of
Macedonian type and cloak draped over his
shoulders.

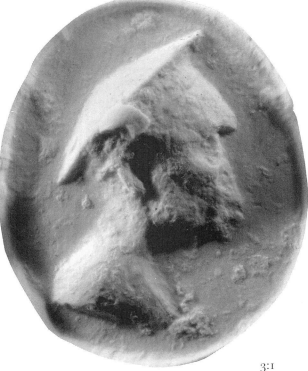

3:1

2:1

**31**                                              3:1

Much of the surface detail is lost through
corrosion and features are barely recognizable.
The head is engraved very deeply into the bezel
and at one point where the metal is thin the iron
has corroded right through. There are horizontal
parallel lines round the band or *stephane* of the
*kausia*, perhaps indicating a diadem, but there are
no ties.

This massive Hellenistic ring with spreading
shoulders is of Egyptian/Ptolemaic type and can
be dated to the 3rd–2nd century BC. Many
Ptolemaic portraits appear on rings like this but
examples are usually found in gold or bronze;
iron is less usual – probably because of the
perishable nature of the material.

The following rings are bronze but of similar shape and are dated to the 3rd century BC: *Oxford 1*, no.287, p.81 (=*GGFR*, pl.815) – it is suggested that these rings may have served some special function at court ceremonial and that those with royal portraits may have been owned by privileged individuals; and O. Neverov, 'A Group of Hellenistic Bronze Rings in the Hermitage', *Vestnik Drevnei Istorii* 127 (1974) pp.106–15, figs.1–29 – these rings from the North Black Sea area were probably brought by traders and are evidence of the spread of Egyptian cults in the region. There are also a few iron rings of the same type: M.-L. Vollenweider, *Die Porträtgemmen der römischen Republik* (1972–74) pl.39.12 (25 × 21.5mm) – a portrait of an unbearded man; *Getty*, nos.79,83–4,87 – all dated to the 4th century BC.

The *kausia* has been traditionally associated with the royal house of Macedonia and in the mid 4th century BC a *kausia* is possibly worn by the rider on Philip II's coins (see P. Dintsis, *Hellenistische Helme*, pl.80.2, p.40, n.177). The *kausia* has sometimes been confused with the *petasos* and is identified with various types of headgear (see Dintsis, *op.cit.* pls.80–3). No actual example has survived but lately there has been much discussion on all aspects of the *kausia* based on archaeological and literary evidence (see A.M. Prestianni Giallombardo 'Un Copricapo dell'Equipaggiamento Militare Macedone: la *Kausia*', *Numismatica e Antichità Classiche* 22 (1993) pp.61–9 and C. Saatsoglou-Paliadeli, 'Aspects of Ancient Macedonian Costume', *JHS* 113 (1993), pp.122–47). It seems probable that the true *kausia* is shown in the type of cap worn by two figures in the lion-hunting scene on the fresco from Tomb II at Vergina (M. Andronikos, *Vergina* (1984) pp.102–3; =Giallombardo, *op.cit.*, pl.2.7, pl.3.8–9; C. Saatsoglou-Paliadeli, *op.cit.*, pl.3b & p.135, fig.3). Here the *kausia* is mushroom-shaped without a brim and made of a single piece of flexible material – probably leather lined with felt. It has a *stephane* around which a diadem could have been worn by royal persons, or without a diadem by others. Apart from the king, it was probably at first worn only by the Royal Pages (who protected him in battle and served as his bodyguards), high-ranking officers, and other specially chosen individuals. After Alexander's death, Ptolemy, Seleukos and others who had served as royal pages in Philip II's court retained the right to wear the *kausia*; portraits of them and others appear on Hellenistic clay bullae, rings (see above) and coins.

It appears that under their rule the *kausia* spread to outlying areas but eventually took on a variety of different forms. Sometimes, like the Bactrian examples, they are far removed from the prototype: Bactria had been conquered by Alexander the Great and for a while was part of the Seleucid kingdom and so Bactrian kings are shown on their coins wearing a version of the *kausia*, see: G. Richter, *Portraits of the Greeks* 3 (1965) pp.278–9, fig.1978 – a rare coin of Demetrius II, ca.190 BC or later; unbearded. (Also fig.1984 – Antimachos I Theos but this is less like the Exeter head.)

The portrait on the Exeter ring is perhaps closer to types on two clay bullae – the first (a) is bearded and probably Seleucid, the second (b) Ptolemaic and typically unbearded:

(a) Clay bulla from Seleucia dated second half of 3rdc. BC–first half of 2ndc. BC; draped bust of a man with long beard, curly hair and wearing a *kausia diadematophoros* (Giallombardo, *op.cit.*, p.89, pl.3.12 =Centro Ricerche Archeologiche e Scavi di Torino . . . *the Land Between Two Rivers* . . . (1985) p.176, no.104; bullae nos.103,105–6 show portraits with deepset eye and heavy brow). (Bearded portraits are unusual at this time but the Seleucid ruler Demetrios II Nikator (161–125 BC) wore a long beard in his second reign (129–125 BC) after his release from imprisonment by the Parthians.)

(b) Clay bulla from Edfu in Egypt, with a portrait of a beardless man with curly hair wearing the *kausia diadematophoros*. He has a heavy brow, deepset eye and prominent chin and resembles portraits of Ptolemy I Sotor, the founder of the Ptolemaic dynasty and king of Egypt 323–285 BC (D. Plantzos, 'Female Portrait Types from the Edfu Hoard of Clay Seal Impressions', in M.-F. Boussac & A. Invernizzi (eds.), *Archives et sceaux du monde hellénistique*, *Turin 1993 (BCH Suppl. 29* (1996) pp.307–13, pl.48.1 (=Allard Pierson, inv.no.8177–230)). On coin types, however, Ptolemy is shown without the *kausia* and with his hair pushed back on his forehead behind a diadem. (Three other clay bullae from Edfu show portraits of men wearing the *kausia*: J.G. Milne, 'Ptolemaic Seal Impressions', *JHS* 26 (1916) p.87ff., nos.63–4 – identified with Ptolemy I Sotor (unbearded), no.65 – perhaps Philadelphus, with traces of a beard(?).)

For portraits (but all unbearded) wearing the *kausia* on gems see:

*Naples*, no.181, pl.15 – glass cameo 26 × 20; a draped bust of a thick-set man ('a Hellenistic prince') wearing a *kausia* of similar type. From Herculaneum.

*Munich* iii, no.3525 – glass paste; 'Hellenistic Macedonian'.

Greek, 3rd–2nd century BC

**32**   5/1946.383 (Montague no.239, p.22)
Ex coll. Prince Hugo Erba Odescalchi (see p.132)

**Ringstone** (F.1?), cornelian, polished surface but chipped on the upper edge.
19 × 13 × 3mm
Mount: late 18th century gold ring, ht.21 × w.24mm; open back, depth of bezel 4mm; plano-convex hoop 2–3mm and the shoulders decorated with double C-scrolls inlaid with a seed pearl on either side.

Publ.: *Bazaar*, 4/1/08, p.66, fig.10.2; (see **pl.b**)

*Draped bust of a bearded god (Zeus?) or man*, in profile to the right wearing a head-band.

4:1

**32** (see also front cover)     4:1     3:1

Montague remarks that this high-quality gem is 'finely cut in the style of the Greek artists employed during the first half of the Roman Empire' (*Bazaar, loc.cit.*). This gem, in Hellenistic Roman style, can be dated to the 1st century BC.

The stone has been chipped at the top and reworked. It was obviously put in its present setting after it was damaged as the gold surround fits the chipped edge. The setting is late 18th century and basically of the simple 'Roman' type (S. Bury, *Rings* (1984) pp.10–11, pl.9) with the addition of double C-scrolls with a seed-pearl set below on either shoulder (compare *Koch*, nos.1045–6,1282 for variants).

The god has an intense expression with parted lips, deepset eye and heavy brow. The eye is shown as three short straight grooves (see also *F.Berlin*, no.3180 and *Ionides*, no.25 below). His hair is engraved in short, irregular curved parallel grooves falling in softer waves below his head-band; his beard is shown by shorter, straighter strokes. Hair styles engraved in similar fashion appear on a number of coins of the 1st century BC and on a gem with Victory by Pamphilos (*Hermitage Intaglios*, no.85).

The youthful, aesthetic head on the Exeter gem cannot be identified with any particular god and appears younger than the usual bearded and long-haired father/god types (Zeus, Serapis, Asklepios and Poseidon). These gods were derived from Pheidias' famous statue of Zeus at Olympia and closely resemble each other but can usually be identified by their attributes. (Compare heads of Zeus and other gods on Hellenistic and Roman Republican coins from the 3rd century BC, M.H. Crawford, *Roman Republican Coinage* 2 vols. (1984) no.44ff. and O. Mørkholm, *Early Hellenistic Coinage: from the Accession to the Peace of Apamea (336–188BC)* (1991) pl.12.206).

Serapis is often draped in this fashion but the youthful head and unclassical profile are certainly uncharacteristic. The gem is chipped where the *modius* (corn measure) would have been and, although on some examples it is very small (*Vienna* I, nos.202, 452; *BMC* Alexandria, no.253 (=Hornbostel, *Sarapis*, no.348 – *diabolon* of Vespasian AD 70/1), it is unlikely that on a gem of this quality the artist would have left so little space (cf.**33–4**).

Compare:

*Ionides*, no.15 – 3rd–2ndc. BC amethyst; probably Poseidon or a 'father/god' type in the Classical tradition.

no.25 – 1stc. BC convex cornelian; a herm bust with a bearded head wearing a fillet; although the hair style is different, the head is very similar to the Exeter example: the engraving of the brow and profile is very close and the eye is shown as three grooves in exactly the same way.

*Cambridge*, no.171 – 1stc. BC Augustan copy of a bearded head of the more usual Early Classical type.

1st century BC gem in an 18th century ring

**33**    5/1946.387 (Montague no.244, p.22)

**Cameo**, glass imitating turquoise.
10 × 9mm
Mount: 18th century gold ring, ht.24 (inc. bezel) × w.21mm; plano-convex hoop; polygonal bezel with closed convex back; ornate shoulders.

Publ.: *Bazaar*, 4/1/08, p.66, fig.10.3; (see **pl.b**).

*Facing head of Zeus/Jupiter-Serapis* wearing a small *modius* or corn measure.

**33**   (see also frontispiece)                                              4:1

4:1

2:1

about a century ago) there is nothing to prove its antiquity, although it has every appearance of authenticity, and was purchased with a guarantee.'

There are not many examples of engraved gems in real turquoise and only a few made of glass imitating turquoise seem to have survived. Pliny, however, when discussing turquoise remarks that '. . . no gemstone is more easily counterfeited by means of imitation in glass' (*Natural History*, 37.33 (Loeb ed. 1962 trans. D.E. Eichholz)). Imitation turquoise was made in different ways and of various materials (G. Devoto & A. Molayem, *Archeogemmologia* (1990) p.112). Besides the Medusa cameo in Leiden mentioned above, other examples of glass turquoise gems appear in: *Geneva* 2, no.61 – first third of 2ndc. BC, a cameo in high relief with a facing bust of Ptolemaic queen; *Vienna* 2, no.821 – a portrait of Vespasian ca.AD 70.

The ring setting is probably early 18th century. Although the polygonal bezel (which doesn't fit the gem) could be late 17th century, the convex underside of the bezel, the split shoulder with the leaf motif and the round silver cup settings are characteristic of the early 18th century (compare *Koch*, nos.792–3).

At the end of the 4th century BC Ptolemy I introduced the worship of Serapis in Egypt as a means of unifying Greeks and Egyptians. Serapis became assimilated to Zeus/Jupiter and together with Isis (**42**) and Harpocrates he formed part of the Alexandrian divine triad. Serapis (or Osiris-Apis) embodied Osiris for the Egyptians and Zeus for the Greeks. He was regarded as a fertility god and is portrayed as a bearded Zeus-type wearing the *modius* (or corn measure of Egypt), a symbol of fertility. He was a popular god whose cult spread to the Greek and Roman world from Egypt during the Hellenistic period. Serapis worship spread from Sicily to Italy and is attested in Rome in 138 BC. (The god had appeared on a Sicilian coin dated after 241 BC.) Heads or busts of Serapis continued on coinage throughout the Imperial era and were also very common on gems – though the profile rather than the frontal view became more usual in the Imperial period (**34**). For a study of the cult, literature and representations of Serapis on coins, gems and in sculpture etc. see *Naples*, pp.6–7; Hornbostel, *Sarapis* (gems no.61ff.); A. Adriani, *Repertorio d'arte dell'Egitto greco-romano*, Seria A ii, pl.75ff. (sculpture).

This fine head of Serapis in late Hellenistic style probably dates to the 1st century BC. A facing head of Medusa on a *phalera* (medallion) in moulded turquoise glass has a very similar appearance and is particularly close in style; it is, though, rather larger and dated slightly later – to the 1st century AD (M. Brouwer, *Glas uit de Oudheid* (1991) pp.32–4 (Leiden, no.VF*522))

Montague (*loc.cit.*) thought the stone was genuine turquoise but may have had doubts about its antiquity as he writes it was '. . . probably cut by a Greek artist during the early Roman Empire; but as the stone has been reset in gold (apparently

For facing heads of Serapis on gems see:

*Ionides*, no.24 – 1stc. BC convex garnet; similar facing head of Serapis related to the 'Zeus Otricoli' type.

*Dalmatian Gems*, no.34 – sealing from a convex cornelian, 1stc. AD.

*Cambridge*, no.545 – late Hellenistic(?) translucent, blue glass cameo pendant with bearded head.

    1st century BC gem in an 18th century ring

**34**  5/1946.714 (Montague no.569, p.56) From William Green (see pp.131–2)

**Ringstone** (F.1), (dark reddish) cornelian ('sard') in very good condition, small chip on edge, polished surface; (?traces of gold leaf in the beard).
13 × 10 × 3mm

*Draped bust of bearded Zeus/Jupiter-Serapis* in profile to the right wearing a *modius* and head-band.

4:1

**34**                     4:1

Profile busts of Serapis were common on gems and coins throughout the Imperial era and under Hadrian (AD 117–38) the cult became especially popular in Rome. (See also the facing head of Serapis, **33**.)

The profile type is common on gems:

T.W. Kibaltchitch, *Gemmes de la Russie Méridionale* (1910) pl.6.205 – cornelian; a good parallel.

*Hague*, no.648 – cornelian; rather more cursory in the 'Imperial Classicising Stripy style' of 1st–2ndc. AD.

*Romania*, no.106 – red jasper.

*Dalmatian Gems*, no.32 – sealing of a gem with a bevelled edge; very similar in style and quality; also nos.33–4.

*Gaul*, no.16 – 1stc. AD flat sard.

*Cologne*, no.365 – 2ndc. AD red jasper in ring.

Hornbostel, *Sarapis*, no.100 (Archaeological Museum, Florence, no.15426) – sardonyx with bevelled edge.

*Cambridge*, no.310 – 2ndc. AD cornelian, small grooves style; quite similar; also nos.309, 311.

    1st–2nd century AD

A Roman version of the 4th century BC head type of Zeus-Serapis. Details are carefully shown with fine wheel grooves. This belongs to the Classicizing style of the 1st–2nd century AD. A number of glass gems have traces of gold leaf left in the device (e.g. *Getty*, p.145 & nos.412, 419,420).

**35** 5/1946.715 (Montague no.570, p.56)
From William Green (see pp.131–2)

**Ringstone** (F.1), pale cornelian; good condition, slight scratching on surface.
11 × 9 × 3mm

*Bust of a bearded god (Zeus or Poseidon?)* in profile to the right; he wears a fillet, has his hair in a roll round his head and two locks falling down his neck; his beard is long and pointed, his lips parted and his eye wide and staring.

**35**                                          4:1

Asklepios; and, as he wears a plain fillet rather than a laurel or ivy wreath round his head, he cannot represent Zeus or Dionysos. However, Dionysian subjects including masks and portraits are often engraved in this style.

There are a number of similar archaizing heads of this type (mostly herm-busts) see:

*Naples*, no.185 – cornelian from Pompeii; a bearded, laureate bust engraved in very similar style and technique.
*Munich* ii, no.937 – 1stc. BC flat nicolo; herm bust.
*Hanover*, no.492 – second half 1stc. BC flat nicolo; 'bearded god' wearing a fillet.
　　nos.490–1 – second half of 1stc. BC convex cornelians; Dionysos/Bacchus(?) herm busts of bearded gods.
*Vienna* 1, no.158 – 1stc. BC cornelian (F.1); herm bust of bearded god (Jupiter Terminalis?).
*Cologne*, no.23 (=Henkel, pl.7, no.117) – 1stc. BC nicolo; classicizing herm bust of Dionysos.
　　no.372 – second half 1stc. BC sardonyx; herm bust of 'laureate god' in slightly archaizing style with hair knotted behind.
*Münzen und Medaillen A.G.*, Basel, 19–20 June 1964, pl.38.635 – 1stc. BC slightly convex cornelian, herm bust of Zeus, bearded and laureate; fine example, similar type and hair style.
G. Platz-Horster, *Die antiken Gemmen aus Xanten 2* (1994) no.111 – 1stc. AD cornelian, 'Zeus'; close to the Exeter gem but rather more cursory; cf. also no.110.

1st century BC–AD 30

The god's hair style drawn with straight parallel wheel grooves, his large wide-open eye and the engraving of the nose and mouth are characteristic of the 'Republican Wheel style' dated from the 1st century BC–AD 30 (*Hague*, pp.154–5).
　　There is no attribute here to identify this god with any particular deity such as Neptune or

**36**   5/1946.712 (Montague no.567, p.56)
From William Green (see pp.131–2)

**Ringstone**   (F.1),   rock   crystal   (or
'chalcedony'); good condition, small chips
round the edge.
10 × 8 × 3mm

*Athena/Minerva* stands frontally with her head
in profile to the left wearing a plumed
Corinthian helmet; her left leg is straight and
her right leg bent; she wears a long belted
*peplos* with overfold; her left arm is raised to
hold the spear which stands upright beside
her and she places her right hand on her
shield which rests on the ground beside her.
In the field on the left are a wreath and palm
branch. Groundline.

standing in numerous positions with many
different combinations of attributes. Apart from
her weight being on the other leg, Athena
appears on the gem itself (but not on the
impression) almost exactly as she does on a gold
coin of Galba dated AD 68 (see *LIMC* ii,
Athena/Minerva, no.113). The palm and wreath
in the field seem unusual – these attributes are
usually carried by a small Victory, often held out
on Athena's hand (e.g. *Vienna* 1, no.180).

There are a number of very close parallels –
though on some examples the motif is in reverse:

*Bonn*, no.1 – 2ndc. AD cornelian in a bronze ring.
*Aquileia*, no.134 – flat red jasper but very cursory
   with little detailing.
F.*Berlin*, no.7228 – Imperial flat cornelian.
*Munich* iii, no.2479 (*LIMC* ii, Athena/Minerva,
   no.104; Henkel, no.421, pl.75.110) – 2nd–3rdc.
   AD flat cornelian in a silver ring.
*Hanover*, no.778 – 1st–2ndc. AD flat cornelian in
   similar style.
*Cologne*, no.260 – 2nd–3rdc. AD cornelian set in
   3rdc. AD ring.

2nd–3rd century AD

**36**   (see also frontispiece)                4:1

The folds of Athena's *peplos* are drawn with thin
parallel lines which run diagonally over her bent
leg to give a stripy or patterned effect in the
Classicizing style of the 2nd–3rd century AD.
   This is a variation on the Athena Parthenos
type (see *LIMC* ii, Athena, no.220). The goddess
was a very popular motif on gems and is shown

**37** 5/1946.385 (Montague no.241, p.22)
Ex coll. Sir Arthur Evans; from Burnum,
Dalmatia (see p.131)

**Ringstone** (F.1), cornelian (yellowish) in
good condition with polished surface; small
chip on right upper edge.
14 × 12 × ca.3mm
Mounted on Evans's blue velvet board with a
sealing wax impression and handwritten
label. (See back cover.)

Publ.: *Bazaar*, 6/4/07, pp.981–2; *Dalmatian
Gems*, Addendum p.169.

*Hermes/Mercury* standing in frontal position
turning slightly to the left with his head in
profile; his right leg is straight and his left leg is
bent; he carries his money bag in his right
hand and has his *caduceus* on his left; his cloak
(*chlamys*) is draped across his torso and is
wrapped round his left arm with the end
hanging down beside him; he wears his winged
hat (*petasos*) and his winged boots. Groundline.

4:1

**37** (see also back cover)                    4:1

This is an exceptionally fine example of a
common motif which is most often very cursorily
drawn (cf. **56–7**). Mercury's graceful, smooth
body is softly and accurately modelled; the details
of his anatomy are carefully engraved and the
drapery across his body seems light and
transparent. The gem belongs to the Imperial
Classicizing style of the 1st century AD. (For the
*petasos* shown in this fashion see *Hague*, no.1017.)

This type of standing Mercury with purse and
*caduceus* was derived from a Greek statuary type of
the 5th and 4th centuries BC and is very common
on gems, metalwork and a variety of other objects.
Mercury was widely venerated as the messenger of
the gods, the guide and protector of travellers, the
guardian of flocks and herds, the patron of
merchants and soldiers – and sometimes also
thieves. He was particularly popular from the
1st–3rd centuries AD in the Western provinces
including Britain (see the rather later and more
usual cursory types found in Exeter (**56–7**) which
belong to Henig's distinctive Flavian group dated
to the end of the 1st–the early 2nd century AD).

Besides **56–7**, compare:

*Aquileia*, no.165 – end of 1stc. BC–early 1stc. AD
flat cornelian; quite close to the Exeter gem;
also nos.166–86, pp.137–8 for the motif.
*Hague*, nos.499–500 – 1stc. AD Classicizing style.
nos.586–7 – 1stc. AD Classicizing style.
*Luni*, no.64 – 1st–2ndc. AD biconvex cornelian.
I.N. Svoronos, 'Katalogos Dorea K. Karapanou,
Sylloge glypton lithon', *Journal International
d'Archéologie Numismatique* 15 (1913) no.152ff. –
good quality gems.
*Romania*, no.236 – cornelian.
*Cologne*, no.256 – 1stc. AD slightly convex 'yellow agate'.
no.257 – 2ndc. AD with winged boots.
*Dalmatian Gems*, no.57 – 1st–2ndc. AD sealing with
bevelled obverse edge.
*Getty*, no.256 – 1stc. AD banded agate (C.4);
winged boots and cap of similar style.

1st century AD

**38**   5/1946.384 (Montague no.240, p.22)
Ex coll. Sir Arthur Evans; from Epidaurum,
Dalmatia (see p.131)

**Ringstone** (F.4?), red jasper; slight wear on
surface, chipped on upper edges.
ca.17 × 12 × 4mm overall
15 × 11mm intaglio face
Mounted on Evans's blue velvet board with a
sealing wax impression and handwritten
label. (See back cover.)

Publ.: *Bazaar*, 6/4/09, pp.981–2, fig.16;
*Dalmatian Gems*, no.86, & Addendum p.169.

*Eros/Cupid* is seated on a pile of rocks in
profile facing to the right playing the double
flute or *tibiae*; a tree spreads over the scene
from behind him on the left. Groundline.

4:1

**38**  (see also back cover)                    4:1

A finely engraved gem in the Imperial
Classicizing style of the 1st–2nd century AD.
Cupid's fat, rounded body is carefully drawn and
details shown with fine grooves.

Cupid is often shown playing the flute but he is
usually walking or standing (compare *Munich* iii,

no.2286; or *Hanover*, no.1467 – a more complex
scene of pastoral sacrifice). For Cupid as a
musician see R. Stuveras, *Le Putto dans l'art romain*,
Collection Latomus 99 (Brussels: 1969) p.104; and
for the double flute see M. Henig, 'A Roman
Intaglio from Chichester', *Ant.Jnl.* (1978) pp.374–7,
and especially A. Wardle, 'A Note on the *Tibiae*',
*ibid.* pp.376–7, pl.76 – a plasma gem with seated
Marsyas and *tibiae*.

This scene with Cupid seated seems unusual but
compare:

*London*, no.2877 – Greco-roman glass gem; a
    similar scene with Cupid sitting under a tree
    playing a lyre but he faces the tree-trunk.
*Vienna* 1, nos.432–3 – end of 1stc. BC–early 1stc.
    AD convex glass gems; different in style but
    seated Cupid plays a double flute in front of a
    herm of the young Dionysos.
*Hague*, no.900 – 1st–2ndc. AD; a cursory example
    with Cupid squatting and playing the double
    flute.
*GGFR*,   no.951 – 4thc. BC Greco-Persian
    chalcedony scaraboid; two erotes seated on
    rocks facing each other; one plays the lyre and
    the other the *tibiae*.

1st–2nd century AD

**39**   5/1946.711 (Montague no.566, p.56)
From William Green (see pp.131–2)

**Ringstone**   (F.1),   cornelian;   surface
scratched.
11 × 9 × 3mm

*Eros/Cupid* turns back to fire an arrow from
his bow with his upper half and head in
profile to the right; his lower half is seen from
the front with his left leg bent at the knee and
his right foot in profile; one wing is shown
behind him and part of the further wing
appears in front of his face. Groundline.

**39**                                4:1

a similar cursory style. The engraving of the head
and feet are close to the Imperial 'Cap-with-Rim'
style dated late 1st–2ndc. AD (*Hague*, p.302ff.)

This was a popular Hellenistic motif dating
back to the 4th–3rd centuries BC and which
continued into Roman times (see *Aquileia*, p.171).

A number of gems show Cupid in various
positions firing his bow:

*Hague*, no.986 – convex cornelian dated 2nd–3rdc.
    AD; a similar Cupid but he is in a slightly different
    position and in the later 'Imperial Incoherent
    Grooves style': see no.981ff., and p.326.
*Aquileia*, no.306 – convex cornelian.
*Britain*, no.135 – 1stc. AD plasma.
*Bari*, no.55 – cornelian, shape F.1; Cupid fires an
    arrow as he moves to the left in profile; a less
    cursory example.
*Luni*, no.59 – 1st–2ndc. AD nicolo paste; a
    different cursory style.
*Getty*, no.320 – 1stc. AD; a fatter Cupid in similar style.

1st–2nd century AD

Cupid is in an unusually complicated position as
he twists round to fire his bow but the engraving is
very cursory with little detailing and is close to the
'Imperial Incoherent Grooves style' (see *Hague*
below). Two figures on gems in *Naples* 1,
nos.203–4, which must date to before AD 79, are in

**40**    4/1946.386 (Montague no.242, p.22)
Ex coll. Sir Arthur Evans; from Scardona,
Dalmatia (see p.131)

**Ringstone** (F.1), cornelian (yellowish orange)
slightly convex face, bevelled edge; fine
scratches on surface.
13 × 10 × ca.3mm
Mounted on Evans's blue velvet board with a
sealing wax impression and handwritten
label. (See back cover.)

Publ.: *Bazaar*, 6/4/07, p.981, fig.16; *Dalmatian
Gems*, Addendum, p.169.

*Two Bacchic figures* (probably *Dionysos/Bacchus
and Ariadne*) riding to the right on a panther
which has its head turned to the front and a
garland round its neck; the figure riding side-
saddle in front leans forward holding a *thyrsos*
with a streamer, while the figure behind
twists round in three quarter view with his
right hand placed on the animal's rump.

**40**  (see also back cover)                         4:1

Details of anatomy are carefully shown with
rounded grooves and the hair with very fine
narrow parallel grooves. The gem belongs to the
Imperial Classicizing style of the 1st–2nd century
AD.

Dionysos/Bacchus or his followers in the *thiasos*
are often shown on gems, sarcophagi and other
objects riding singly on lions or panthers. For
example, a young Dionysos with *thyrsos* rides a
panther on a 1st century BC–1st century AD gem
in *Berlin*, no.378.

The scene on the Exeter gem showing two
figures riding one animal seems unusual but a
version very close to it appears on a well-known
cornelian gem in Florence (see below) – though it
is in a finer style with details shown more clearly.
This suggests that there may have been an
ancient prototype for the scene. (The Florence
gem was evidently copied in the 18th century and
has been published several times – see E.
Zwierlein-Diehl, 'Antikisierende Gemmen des
16.–18. Jahrhunderts' pp.396–8, abb.39–40 in
*PACT* 23 (1989) VI.1 ed. T. Hackens & G.
Moucharte.)

For an 18th century glass copy of the original
cornelian in Florence (inv.1565) see:

*Würzburg* 1, no.231 (=*PACT op.cit.*, abb.41) –
Classicizing style of the end of 1st century
BC–beginning of 1st century AD. Details of
drapery and anatomy are finely engraved and
clearly show a Baccant with a female
companion, or Dionysos/Bacchus and
Ariadne. The only iconographic difference is
that the *thyrsos* is held by the Baccant riding
behind rather than his female companion –
though she still stretches her arm out over the
panther's head. (See refs.)

1st–2nd century AD

**41**   5/1946.358 (Montague no.221, p.20)
From Alexandria

**Ringstone** (F.1), blue glass, iridescent; large chip on upper left edge.
19 × 15 × 4mm

Publ.: *Bazaar*, 13/4/07, p.1055, fig.26.

*Hermanubis*, standing frontally with his right leg straight and left leg bent, faces to the left with his head in profile; he is crowned with a *modius* (and lotus petals?) and wears a *himation* which appears to be draped over one shoulder leaving his torso bare; in his right hand he holds a palm branch and has the winged *caduceus* of Hermes/Mercury on his left; behind him on the right a small dog (or jackal(?), the symbol of Anubis) with one paw raised, turns its head round to face him. Groundline.

4:1

**41**   (see also frontispiece)   4:1

Hermanubis is the anthropomorphic and Hellenized form of the Egyptian jackal-headed god Anubis (see **54**). In Egypt in the 2nd and 3rd centuries Hermes and Anubis were syncretized as they played parallel roles as *psychopompi* – both were thought to conduct the souls of the dead to the world beyond. Anubis appears frequently on magic gems, often carrying the palm and *caduceus*, the attributes of Hermes and Hermanubis (see *Kassel*, no.143, *Merz*, no.235). Hermes also had an important role on magic gems (see Delatte/ Derchain, no.229, Hermes in his pure form with a magic inscription).

Hermanubis is shown on a number of statues and statuettes, as well as on numerous Alexandrian coins of the 2nd and 3rd centuries AD (see *LIMC* v, Hermanubis, pp.265–7). His dog is sometimes supposed to be a jackal and his *modius* often has a lotus petal in front and at the side – (on the Exeter gem details are not clear); all have bare torsos.

The motif seems unusual on gems but common on coins, compare:

*BMC* Alexandria, no.2050 – a coin of Philippus II (AD 244–7); the closest parallel to the gem; he wears a *modius* and has a *himation* of the same length draped over his shoulder and lower limbs; a palm on his right and *caduceus* on his left; the dog or jackal.
no.1138 – a coin of Antoninus Pius (AD 138–61); he holds a palm on his right hand and *caduceus* on his left; the jackal is on the right and looks

back towards him. (For a similar type see *LIMC* v, Hermanubis, no.7.)

no.1428 – a coin of Commodus (AD 180–93) as above but the other way round and his *caduceus* is winged.

*Sofia*, no.53 – convex cornelian; probably Hermanubis but uncertainly identified as Apollo(?) with a dog, palm and a 'bow' which appears more like a *caduceus*.

2nd–3rd century AD

**42**   5/1946.713 (Montague no.568, p.56)
From William Green (see pp. 131–2)

**Ringstone** (F.1), red jasper; slightly scratched on the surface, chip on upper right edge.
12 × 8 × 3mm

*Draped Bust of Isis* (or a woman wearing her hair in Isiac fashion) in profile to the right; her hair is in a roll round her head and gathered into a bun low on her neck with one long corkscrew ringlet hanging down the side of her neck and another down her back; she is wearing a light *himation* draped across her chest and tied in a *nodus Isiacus* in front.

4:1

**42**                                              4:1

Her face, neck and shoulders are drawn with wide, smooth grooves and details of features outlined with wheel grooves; her hair is shown by straight parallel lines. M.-L. Vollenweider has dated red jasper portraits of this type to the Antonine period in the second half of the 2nd century AD when private individuals copied portraits of Faustina II and her daughters (see *Geneva 2*, no.242 below).

The cult of the Alexandrian divine triad (Isis, Serapis (**33–4**) and Harpocrates) spread throughout the Roman Empire but by the Antonine period it had become especially popular in Rome. It seems likely that this jasper gem represents a private individual who belonged to the cult of the goddess, rather than an image of the goddess herself. Although the hair style and *himation* tied in a *nodus Isiacus* are typical of Isis, on other gems, statuettes, busts, coins etc. she usually also wears her distinctive emblem or lotus crown (see coins of the 1st–3rd centuries AD: *LIMC* v, 'Isis', no.102ff.; *BMC Alexandria*, pl.16.303,2029, 2268) – though an exception does appear on a relief from Cerveteri (*LIMC* v, 'Isis', no.135 – Os, Brussels, Mus.Roy. R 1515).

For busts of Isis and portraits of similar type to the Exeter jasper gem see:

*Journal of the Walters Art Gallery* 47 (1989), J. Speir 'A Group of Ptolemaic Engraved Garnets', pp.21–38, Fig.3 (Walters Art Gallery no.42.1106) – 2nd–1stc. BC garnet showing bust of Isis with Libyan locks, head-dress and *himation* tied in a *nodus Isiacus*.

*Getty*, no.208 – a mid 1stc. BC cornelian (F.1); a Ptolemaic queen as Isis with Libyan locks and the lotus crown.

no.330 – 2nd–3rdc. AD nicolo (F.2); a head of a woman engraved in very similar style but without ringlets.

*London*, no.3619 – a cameo portrait of an empress as Isis wearing the crown and *nodus Isiacus*.

*LIMC* v, 'Isis', no.176 (Staatl.Mus.Ägypt. Mus.9822) – 2ndc. AD full length figure of Isis showing her with a similar hair style but wearing the crown.

*Geneva* 2, no.242 – red jasper, ca.AD 165; draped bust of a woman with a similar hair style but with short strands of hair hanging down her neck rather than ringlets.

Second half of the 2nd century AD

**43**   5/1946.391 (Montague no.247, p.23)

**Ringstone** (F.2 or 4?), red jasper; good condition bronze ring with traces of gilding.
14 × 11mm overall (including bevelled edge)
13 × 10mm intaglio face
Mount: bronze ring, ht.19 × w.22mm (interior diam. 14 × 12mm) with traces of gilding; plano-convex hoop.

Publ.: *Bazaar*, 28/12/07, p.1861, fig.8

*Draped Bust of a Bearded Man* in profile to the right wearing a diadem.

4:1

**43**                                               4:1

2:1

The engraving is rather cursory and linear with parallel rounded grooves for the hair and beard. Although in some ways this bust resembles gems which have been dated 16th–17th century and a group in Bari considered doubtful, the Exeter bronze ring appears ancient and, although the stone is not necessarily contemporary with the ring, it appears to fit well into the setting. (Compare *Vienna* 3, no.2694 – 16th–17thc. jasper, F.1; *Bari*, no.99ff. – though these are all engraved in cornelian and are shape F.3; see also the discussion *Luni*, no.100.) This portrait suggests a foreigner and could well be provincial work – perhaps from the East.

The odd-shaped head, hair style, diadem and even the linear drapery bear a remarkable resemblance to portraits on coins of the Bactrian ruler Strato I. These coins are dated to the end of his reign, ca.80–75 BC (see A.K. Narain, *The Indo-Greeks* (1957) pl.3, nos.7–12) and show him as an old man with prominent brow and beardless(?) jutting chin. (On an earlier coin *op.cit.* pl.3, no.4) he is shown bearded.)

The ring is massive and although its form corresponds to types of the 2nd century AD (cf. Henkel, pl.32,802–3, pl.35,923), the interior diameter of the hoop is so small that it could be worn only on the upper joint of a little finger; it would have been more suitable for suspension.

The portrait seems unusual but compare:

Richter 2, no.62 (Paris, CM, Chabouillet, no.1418) – agate; a similar portrait type ('head of Jupiter') wearing *taenia* and draped in a mantle. (It has been suggested that this may not be ancient.)

2nd century AD

**44**  5/1946.436 (Montague no.292, p.27)

**Cameo pendant**, glass (yellowish beige); with a raised border; the tab with hole for suspension broken off.
18 × 16 × ca.3mm (impressed surface 15 × 13mm)

*Facing profile draped busts* of a man on the right and woman on the left; possibly imperial.

Glass medallions such as this with portraits or other motifs are quite common. Couples probably exchanged portrait medallions of this sort on betrothal. It is often difficult to know whether the portraits are of imperial couples or private individuals who imitated imperial hair styles.

On this medallion the man has short curly hair and there are signs of a short beard; the woman wears her hair looped low on her neck in Severan fashion. The portraits rather resemble those of Caracalla and his wife Plautilla though she was empress only from AD 202–205 (see S. Nodelman, 'A Portrait of the Empress Plautilla' in *The J. Paul Getty Mus. Jnl.* 10 (1982) p.105ff.).

Compare:

A.B. Chadour, *Schmuck II, Fingerringe* (1985) no.90 – cornelian intaglio with facing profile portraits of Caracalla and Plautilla (AD 202–205).
*Geneva 2*, no.262 – brown glass medallion with facing profile portraits of a man and a woman similar to those on the Exeter medallion; Vollenweider suggests they may portray Philip the Arab and his wife Otacilia; dated AD 244–268.

3rd century AD

**44**                                    4:1

**45**   5/1946.388 (Montague no.243, p.22)
Ex coll. Sir Arthur Evans; from Istria? (see p.131)

**Ringstone** (C.3 or 4), cornelian (orange).
12 × 10 × ca.4mm
Mount: modern metal surround.

Publ.: *Bazaar*, 6/4/07, p.982, fig.17; *Dalmatian Gems*, no.136, Addendum p.169.

*Pegasus* flying to the right.

**45**   (see also frontispiece)         4:1

half of the 1st century BC–AD 30 (*Hague*, pp.179–80 and nos.424ff.).

Winged horses appeared very early on gems and there are many examples of Pegasus on coins and gems from the Greek Classical period onwards. The motif appeared on Roman coins from the 3rd century BC and was particularly common on late Republican and early Imperial gems (see Kent, *RC*, pl.14.43 – denarius). Pegasus was the emblem of the *gens* Titius and so the moneyer Quintus Titius had Pegasus and Q. Titi stamped on the reverse of his coins in about 90 BC. On some examples a male head on the obverse is identified as Mutinus Titinus (Priapus) and Montague points out there could be a further allusion here because of the close resemblance between this name and Q. Titi (*Bazaar*, *loc.cit.*; E.A. Sydenham, *The Coinage of the Roman Republic* (1952), pl.20.691 – denarius (88 BC), Pegasus and Q. Titi on the reverse and head of Mutinus Titinus on the obverse).

On gems see:

B.Y. Berry, *Ancient Gems from the collection of Burton Y. Berry*, no.27 – Classical Greek sardonyx.
*N.Y.*, no.395 – 4thc. BC type; convex cornelian.
*Munich* ii, no.797 – 2ndc. BC convex cornelian.
*F.Berlin*, no.2344–5 – early Roman convex amethyst and cornelian.
*London*, no.1850 – convex cornelian.
*Hanover*, no.1136 – 1stc. AD; similar in style; also nos.1134ff.
D. Sturdy & M. Henig, *The Gentle Traveller*, p.4.b – convex red cornelian (Canterbury Cathedral Library: Bargrave Collection).
*Getty*, no.299 – 1stc. AD convex amethyst (A.4); similar.

1st century BC

Convex gems deeply engraved with rounded forms like this somewhat heavy-weight Pegasus are characteristic of the 1st century BC and are reminiscent of the earlier 'Campanian- and Hellenistic-Roman styles'; also compare this Pegasus with the animals in Maaskant's 'Republican Flat Bouterolle style' dated second

**46**  5/1946.394 (Montague no.250, p.23)

**Ringstone** (F.3), cornelian; good condition.
7 × 5 × ca.3mm
Mount: ancient silver ring (ht.20 × w.19mm);
hoop triangular in section with projecting,
curved and concave shoulders which rise to a
high bezel; fractured.

Publ.: *Bazaar*, 4/1/08, p.66, fig.10.1; (see
**pl.b**).

A *Fish*

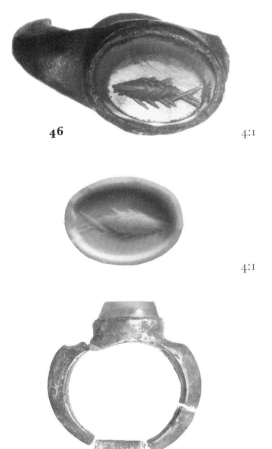

**46**                                            4:1

4:1

2:1

The fish is quite carefully engraved with a
number of fine wheel grooves to indicate tail, fins
and mouth.

This ring is possibly early Christian. Fish had
always been popular motifs, but in the 3rd
century AD a fish was one of the symbols listed by
Clement of Alexandria as suitable for Christians
to have on their rings. He recommended that one
ring only should be worn (*Paedagog*, ii, ch.11; C.W.
King, *Antique Gems and Rings* 1 (1872) pp.329–30).
The Greek name for fish, Ιχθυς, stands for the
first letters of 'Ιησους Χριστος Θεον Υιος
Σωτηρ' = 'Jesus Christ, Son of God, Saviour'.

The ring shape is a common 3rd century AD
type. For similar ring types see *LondonRings*,
fig.86=no.526 (gold); Henkel, pl.48.1260–1,1267–8
(bronze), p.115.

For similar fish – several engraved on truncated
cone-shaped gems (F.3) – see:

*Merz*, no.495 – 1stc. AD cornelian in a gold ring.
*Hague*, no.798 – 1st–2ndc. AD layered agate (F.3).
*Gaul*, no.784 – layered sardonyx (F.3).
*Britain*, app. no.192 – early 3rdc. AD pale
    cornelian (F.3); set in a silver ring (fig.1, type
    V). From Chester.
Henkel, pl.77.280 – 3rdc. AD sard (F.3); a fish
    engraved in very similar style but set in a
    different 3rdc. AD ring type (no.434).
*Getty*, no.396 – 3rdc. AD yellow jasper (F.3) set in a
    3rdc. AD silver ring of different type.

3rd century AD

**47**   5/1946.392 (Montague no.248, p.23)

**Ringstone** (convex), green and white mottled jasper, irregular double bevelled edge, some scratches on the face.
14 × 10mm
Mount: ancient gilded copper alloy (brass or bronze) ring; ht.20 (inc. stone) × w.23; irregular polygonal hoop.

Publ.: *Bazaar*, 21/12/07, p.1779

A *Combination* (or '*gryllos*') of '*hippalectryon*' type walks to the right, composed of a beardless mask with a plain cap and a cock's legs, feet and (?)tail or misunderstood eagle's beak; emerging from the tail/beak and curving over the mask is a small horse's head on a serpent-like neck; standing on the tail/beak is a small animal (a mouse or bird?), holding reins and driving it along. Groundline.

4:1

2:1

**47**  (see also frontispiece)                    4:1

This is engraved with smooth, broad grooves; the nose and mouth are shown as narrow parallel wheel grooves. This mask-animal gem can be related to Maaskant's 'Plain' or 'Imperial Incoherent Grooves style' of the 3rd century AD (*Hague*, p.326).

Rings with polygonal hoops (often more elaborate) date to the 3rd century AD (cf. Henkel, nos.76 (gold), 428 (silver), 931, 1302–3 (bronze), 1386 (copper)). This gem does not fit into the bezel very well and it is possible that the ring and stone did not originally belong together – though they are of about the same date. (For gilding in the Roman period see J. Ogden, *Jewellery of the Ancient World* (1982), pp.78–81.)

Details on the gem are not clear but a horse's head was probably intended, rather than a serpent as Montague suggests (*Bazaar, loc.cit.*; cf. *Vienna 3*, no.2123). The tail resembles an eagle's beak which appears on a related but more complex combination (M. Henig, 'A new combination gem', *Ant. Jnl.* 60, pt.2 (1980) pp.332–3, pl.60,d,e). Combinations date from Phoenician times but the later type came to Rome via Hellenistic Greece. They were worn as magic amulets to ward off the evil eye. (For their origins see *AGGems*, pp.84–5.)

The Exeter *gryllos* is unusual but is basically of '*hippalectryon*' type with elements from other combinations. Compare:

*Britain*, no.382 – a small head (or figure?) behind the horse's neck.

*Hague*, no.1086 – ca.2nd–3rdc. AD onyx; a bearded Silenus mask, cock's body and legs surmounted by a horse's head; a small cupid behind the Silenus's ear.

  no.1087 – ca.2nd–3rdc. AD cornelian; as above but without cupid; the style of engraving (especially the mask profile) is very similar to the Exeter gem.

  no.1093 – ca.2nd–3rdc. AD red jasper; cupid riding a Silenus mask with horse's head over a bird pecking a snake.

*Vienna* 3, no.2120 – 2ndc. AD cornelian; as above but cupid drives the '*hippalectryon*'.

  nos.2117–18 – 2ndc. AD cornelians; a mouse driving ostrich combinations.

2nd–3rd century AD

**48**   5/1946.390 (Montague no.246, p.23)

**Ringstone** (F.), dark green jasper; good condition, some small scratches.
12 × 10mm
Mount: ancient iron ring (corroded) ht.22 × w.25mm (depth of bezel 4mm); plano-convex hoop. (As *Britain*, fig.1, ring type III.)

Publ.: *Bazaar*, 28/12/07, p.1862, fig.9.1

A *Raven* stands on an *altar* on the left of the field; on the right is a *cornucopia* and below it a *dolphin*. Groundline.

**48**  (see also frontispiece)                    4:1

2:1

A carefully engraved gem close to the 'Imperial Small Grooves style' of 1st–2nd century AD (see *Hague*, pp.251–2).

Jasper ringstones are often set in rings of this type which have a plain hoop, though often with slightly projecting shoulders. The type is common in the 2nd century AD (*LondonRings*, p.xlvi, E xvii=no.1156; Henkel, nos.1177,1188–90 (bronze), nos.1534–5 (iron)).

Montague pointed out that these are symbols of prosperity which could represent earth (the cornucopia), air (the bird), fire (the altar) and water (the fish or dolphin) 'and could have been connected with an oath of fidelity taken upon the four elements' (*Bazaar, loc.cit.*). On the other hand, as the bird is a raven it could also be interpreted as the symbol of Apollo, and in turn the altar, dolphin and cornucopia as symbols of Zeus, Neptune and Fortuna.

For similar groups of prosperity symbols (or attributes of deities) compare:

*Vienna* 3, no.1781 – 2ndc. AD nicolo (F.4); the raven of Apollo on a tripod pecking fruit from a cornucopia, a dolphin and trident, and a globe. (Also symbols of earth, air, fire and water?)

*Britain*, no.395 – cornelian; a raven on an altar, a cornucopia and other symbols connected with Apollo.

*Caerleon*, p.129, no.6 – dark green prase (C.1) dated ca.AD 75–85; raven on a *calathus*, corn-ear, cornucopia with globe beneath.

*Nijmegen*, no.130 – ?onyx in 2ndc. AD iron ring of the same type; the raven of Apollo on a tripod flanked by cornucopias.

2nd century AD

**49**   5/1946.393 (Montague no.249, p.23)

**Ringstone** (F), etched cornelian with a chalky-white, crazed upper surface.
12 × 10mm
Mount: ancient iron ring ht.23 × w.24mm (depth of bezel 4mm); plano-convex hoop. (As *Britain*, fig.1, ring type III.)

Publ.: *Bazaar*, 28/12/07, p.1861, fig.8

An *Eagle* in three quarter view to the left with its head facing right stands on an *altar* flanked by two *military standards* and *clasped hands* (*dextrarum iunctio*) below.

**49**

4:1

4:1

2:1

The *Eagle* was a symbol of Zeus, the Emperor, the legions, the Empire and Imperial victory. The eagle sitting on an altar between military standards was naturally a popular subject for soldiers to have on their rings and there are examples on gems from all over the Empire (*Geneva* 2, no.456; *Bari*, nos.69–70.)

The *Dextrarum iunctio* was often used on betrothal rings but from the Republican period in the late 1st century BC it was also used (alone or with other symbols) as a political device on gems and coins. On coins the motif is often accompanied by legends such as 'CONCORDIA EXERCITVVM' or 'FIDES EXERCITVVM' (Kent, *RC*, nos.219,252). (For references to this motif, sometimes with other symbols, on coins and gems see *Naples* 1, p.173; *Aquileia*, no.1489; *Geneva* 2, nos.466–8; *Getty*, no.327.)

On coins from the 1st century BC, the related motif of the *aquila*, the sign of the *aquilifer*, between military standards is much more usual than the eagle on the altar. Compare:

*BMC Empire* 2, pl.12.15 – coin of Vespasian AD 69–70(?) of the 'Concordia Militum' type; clasped hands hold an *aquila* between military standards, perhaps referring to war on the frontiers.

*RIC* 3, pl.9.187 – coin of Marcus Aurelius (ca.AD 176–80); the eagle on an altar (but without the standards).

The following gems are close to the Exeter example but there is no altar:

*Thorvaldsen*, no.1820 – late Roman heliotrope; eagle with head to left holding a wreath and palm branch in its beak, standing on clasped hands between military standards.
*Aquileia*, no.1284 – convex cornelian; similar.

2nd century AD

This gem is engraved with rounded grooves, and details are shown with fine parallel lines. The motif is cut through the upper white layer to the darker layer beneath. The white, crazed upper surface has perhaps been etched intentionally to imitate layered agate or sardonyx and has later become weathered (see M. Sax, 'Recognition and Nomenclature of Quartz Materials with specific reference to Engraved Gemstones', *Jewellery Studies* 7 (1996) pp.66–7; and cf. **95** and **103**). Like **48**, the engraving is related to the 'Imperial Small Grooves style' of the 1st–2nd centuries AD (cf. *Hague*, no.759 – an eagle on an altar with standards). The iron ring is also of the same 2nd century type (cf. Henkel, pl.58.1527, and pl.77.264 (=pl.69.1832 – eagle, altar and standards in a similar 2nd century ring)).

All the symbols on this gem have a military significance and appear, either alone or combined with a variety of other symbols, on coins and other gems:

**50**   5/1946.399 (Montague no.255, p.24)
From Dorchester (Durnovaria), Dorset; found
in or before 1907.

**Bronze ring** with intaglio inscription on the
flat bezel; some corrosion.
17 × 7mm
Ring: ht.17 × w.23mm (depth of bezel 2mm);
hoop ca.2–4mm

Publ.: *Bazaar* 21/12/07, p.1778, fig.4; *RIB* 2, fasc.
iii, 'Brooches, rings, gems . . .' p.30, *RIB* 2422.74.

*'Legionary' ring* with XVII (seventeen) incised;
this is not in reverse and so is to be read from
the ring.

Montague suggested this ring was 'no doubt the
property of a legionary belonging to the 17th
Legion . . . Coins inscribed LEG.XVII and
LEG.XVII.CLASSICAE were struck by Marcus
Antonius, and it is possible that this regiment may
have been quartered in Britain during the 1st or
2nd century.' (*Bazaar, loc.cit.*). However, doubts have
been expressed as to whether the ring was found in
Dorchester as bronze rings with incised numerals
are common outside Britain (see *RIB, loc.cit.*).

For bronze rings of this type see:

*LondonRings*, nos.655ff. and p.xxi.
Henkel, pl.31.770 (unengraved bezel), pl.34.899–90
    (incised 'XXVI' and 'XXXII') p.84 – bronze
    rings of the same shape but slightly heavier.

About 1st–2nd century AD

**50**                                    4:1

2:1

The ring has a flattened bezel wider than the
hoop and slightly flattened shoulders on either
side of it.
   Many bronze rings of this type have been
found around Rome and are known as 'legionary
rings' although the engraved number is
sometimes higher than the number of a legion.
However, the numbers are never greater than a
hundred and so it has been suggested that they
were given out to the soldiers of a *centuria* as a
means of identification (see *LondonRings*, p.xxi).

**51**   5/1946.403 (Montague no.259, p.24)
Found at Alexandria

**Intaglio, silvered iron ring** with engraved motif on the flat bezel.
14 × 11 × 3mm
Ring: ht.20 × w.19mm; plano-convex hoop (bent)

Publ.: *Bazaar*, 21/12/07, p.1779, fig.5.

2:1

*Silvered iron ring* with symbols(?)

**51**                                                          4:1

Montague assigns this ring, found in Alexandria, to the Romano-Egyptian period (30 BC–AD 323). The object engraved on the bezel is difficult to interpret and Montague thought it was possibly a round-bottomed vase in a stand (see *Bazaar, loc.cit.*). It seems more probable that the ring had a protective and apotropaic function and that the motif is a combination of symbols. For a similar ring type see Henkel, no.96 – a gold ring with an engraved figure dated to around the end of the Republic.

The device appears to be a combination of three symbols, two Egyptian and one possibly Roman:

a) The *Ankh* sign represented a sandal strap and could mean 'life', 'welfare' and 'endurance'. It appears in various forms, sometimes with a spreading base (rather resembling the *sa* sign).

b) The *Sa* sign represented a rolled and doubled-over bundle of matting for a shepherd's shelter and so was the hieroglyph for 'protection' on an amulet.

c) The Greek or Roman *Thunderbolt* (here represented by the two bow-like objects) was the attribute of Zeus (see F.*Berlin*, no.8008). (These two bows, though, are also reminiscent of ancient Egyptian boomerangs or 'throw-sticks' used for hunting. Although they do not appear as symbols in Egyptian art, a model of a throw-stick was placed in Tutankhamun's tomb, probably for ritual purposes, and would have had a symbolic and protective significance (see *Treasures of Tutankhamun*, BM exhib. catalogue (1972) no.48).)

The symbols on the ring appear to be bound together by three horizontal bands (the centre groove stippled, the other two plain). This triple tie goes back to the 2nd millennium BC – see E. Gubel, 'La Glyptique et la Genèse de l'Iconographie Monétaire Phénicienne, 1', *Studia*

*Phoenicia* 9 (1992) T. Hackens & G. Moucharte (eds.), pp.5–6, n.30,31 & pl.3,9a–c (pl.3,9c has stippling on the central band in the same way as on the Exeter ring). Both thunderbolts and *ankh* signs are sometimes shown with these grooves – see Andrews, *Jewellery*, no.111, p.128 – an *ankh* on the reverse of a pectoral.

The Egyptian *ankh* and *sa* signs were often used side-by-side in Egyptian art but they were not, to my knowledge, actually combined as they are on this ring (see for example the 'motto clasps', Aldred, *Jewels*, pls.31,44 meaning 'all protection and life', pp.16–17 (=Andrews, *op.cit.*, pl.9,108b, pp.17,125); Delatte/Derchain, pp.367–8.) The Greek or Roman thunderbolt of Zeus and the *ankh* also appear together: on a 3rd century BC Egyptian limestone relief from Tanis in the British Museum, Ptolemy II Philadelphus (d.246 BC) stands with his arm raised behind him wielding what appears to be a thunderbolt while Arsinoe II opposite him holds an *ankh* at her side (J. Quaegebeur, 'Ptolémée II en adoration devant Arsinoé II divinisée', *BIFAO* 69 (1971) p.191ff., pl.28 (=EA 1056)).

The idea of superimposing several symbols of this type seems unusual in Egyptian art but there is a composite faience amulet (dated to the 25th dynasty to Late Period, about 700–500 BC) which is formed of a *djed*, *ankh* and *was* sceptre – symbolic of dominion (see *The British Museum Book of Ancient Egypt* (1992) eds. S. Quirke & J. Spencer, no.74, p.95 (EA 54412); for a similar example, but with *ankh* and *was* only, see Andrews, *Amulets*, pls.64o,89e, p.87 (EA 65539), dated to the New Kingdom).

The Phoenicians combined symbols in a similar way: on the obverse of a Punic coin from Malta with a head of Isis-Astarte (dated after 218 BC), a *caduceus* is conflated with the symbol of Tanit (see Bluma L. Trell, 'Phoenician Greek Imperial Coins', *Israel Numismatic Journal* 6–7 (1982–3), p.128ff., pl.25.25; also G.F. Hill, *Coins of Ancient Sicily* (1903), pl.15.15 – here the Tanit sign is mistaken for an *ankh*). The Egyptian *tyet* sign (Aldred, *op.cit.*, p.16) and the *ankh* have been suggested as prototypes for the Tanit symbol and all three resemble each other. For the Carthaginians symbols did not indicate any specific deity but were all considered sacred and were thus interchangeable (Trell, *op.cit.*, pp.130–1,135).

The combination of Egyptian symbols and the thunderbolt on this ring would have had powerful amuletic properties and perhaps reflect this Phoenicio-Punic tradition.

Romano-Egyptian, about 1st century BC–1st century AD(?)

**52**    5/1946.389 (Montague no.245, p.22)
Found at Nazareth, Galilee

**Cameo**, three-layered agate ('flint'): pinkish white layer/blue-grey, thin irregular layer/mottled blue-grey, beige and white layer; a large chip on the face.
17 × 14 × 11mm

Publ.: *Bazaar*, 13/4/07, p.1055, fig.25

*Medusa mask* seen directly from the front with wings on the top of her head and snakes for hair framing her face and knotted under her chin.

**52**                                              4:1

There is a large chip on the forehead and nose. The cameo could have been set in a ring or as a pendant on a necklace or earrings.

4:1

The Medusa mask was the most common motif on cameos and functioned as an amulet. It had powerful apotropaic qualities and was thought to divert the evil eye from the wearer. This is the 'beautiful pathetic' type of the Medusa Rondanini and frequently appears on buildings, gravestones and mosaics. These heads are difficult to date but Henig suggests that the better gems are earlier and the more stylized examples such as this example are a little later – about 3rd century AD (see *Content Cameos*, pp.87–92).

For Medusa masks see:

*Content Cameos*, no.161 – 3rdc. AD(?) white onyx/chalcedony cameo; rounded face with the head seen directly from the front – very similar stylization of the hair and wings to the Exeter cameo.

*Sa'd*, nos.407–9 – similar cameos dated 1st–2ndc. AD. From near Umm Qeis, Gadara, a Hellenistic and Roman city.

*Britain*, nos.725–31.

*Getty*, no.448 – 2nd to early 3rdc. AD; similar to the Exeter cameo and about the same size. From Asia Minor. (Also nos.446–7.)

*Ionides*, no.73 – a finer Roman example in three quarter view.

no.41 – a Hellenistic garnet intaglio with Medusa.

no.98 – a fine late Renaissance cameo.

About 3rd century AD

**53**  5/1946.356 (Montague no.219, p.20)

**Ringstone** (F.), green jasper; very good condition.
15 × 11mm
Mount: ornate gold ring, probably 19th century, in the style of a 16th–17th century signet ring; ht. (inc. stone) 22 × w.22mm; closed back.

Publ.: *Bazaar*, 16/10/14, p.632, fig.1

'*Pantheistic Bes*' – a bearded figure with double wings, head of the Egyptian god Bes, a falcon's tail combined with a crocodile's tail below it; he is seen frontally with his legs and feet turned to the left; he has four arms, two attached to wings and two free; he holds two sceptres on the left and one on the right and has his fourth arm at his side; he wears the crown of Atef (the crown of Osiris on horns) with a ureus on either side; he appears to have lions' masks on his knees and is possibly ithyphallic; a flail (and sceptre?) (or a balance?) appears beside his leg on the left. Groundline.

**53**                                4:1

4:1

The origin and identity of this gnostic god is obscure. His ancient name is unknown and so he is usually referred to as 'Pantheistic Bes'. There are many variants on this figure, which seems to represent different war gods and was believed to be strongly apotropaic, protecting the wearer from serpents and scorpions. Gems of this sort often had inscriptions round the figure as well as on the back of the gem (here covered by the setting). As the image on the gem was supposed to ward off the evil eye, the stone functioned as an amulet rather than a seal. For the same reason, inscriptions on these amulets were not engraved in reverse but could be read from the stone (see **54**).

Although the engraving here is less cursory than on many gems with this motif, attributes become clearer when the figure is compared with more carefully engraved, complex versions (see Delatte/Derchain, nos.166,168 below and p.126ff.): the rounded grooves projecting on either side of his face are supposed to represent animal heads; three diagonal strokes indicate his beard; the two grooves on his knees probably indicate lions' masks and another his phallus. The object on his right appears to be the sceptre and whip. (His feet are not the usual jackal heads.)

For parallels see:

*Vienna 3*, no.2216 – 2nd (–first half of 3rd?)c. AD; green jasper; very close to the Exeter example. (For the engraving of the anatomy and dating see *Caerleon*, no.64 – dated AD 160–230.)

Delatte/Derchain, no.166 – jasper; a finely engraved version of the god showing many attributes.

no.168 – lapis lazuli; a simpler version than the above but it clearly shows the attributes that appear on the Exeter gem.

*Aquileia*, no.1551 – flat lapis lazuli; p.424 for literature.

*Mira et Magica* (1986) no.178 – 2ndc. AD brown-green jasper (F.1); also nos.176–7,179.

2nd–early 3rd century AD

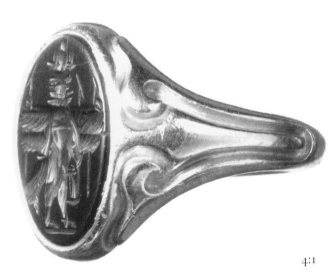

4:1

2:1

**54**  5/1946.355 (Montague no.218, p.20)
'Probably from Alexandria'

**Ringstone** (F.1), obsidian engraved on both
faces (i & ii) and round the bevelled edge (iii, see
p.70); two chips on the upper edge of (i) and
lower right edge of (ii). (Confirmed by SEM
analysis.)
Obverse (i) 18 × 13.5 × 3mm
Reverse (ii) 14 × 10mm

Publ.: *Bazaar* 30/11/06, pp.1477–8, 2 figs.

Obverse (i):
*A rearing serpent with female (or youthful beardless
male?) janiform head* wearing a head ornament
(probably a lotus diadem) with a partly
legible inscription (not retrograde) and one(?)
star in the field.

Reverse (ii):
*Anubis*, the jackal-headed god, stands
unclothed(?) facing left with forearms raised in
gesture of adoration; he appears to have human
or baboon-like hands but a short tail and
jackal's back paws; a partly legible inscription
(not retrograde) and three stars in the field.

**54 (i)**  (see also frontispiece)          4:1          **(ii)**          4:1

The engraving is less cursory than on many magic amulets, with some attention given to detail. The letters and signs, especially on the obverse, are clearly shown and the janiform head is carefully engraved. Thin diagonal parallel lines mark the serpent's body and the jackal's coat. Obsidian (H=5), a volcanic glass, was not often used for seals but there are examples from the Archaic period onwards (6th and early 5th century BC).

As is usually the case on gnostic gems and magic amulets, the inscriptions are to be read from the stone itself rather than from the impression where they appear in reverse. The inscriptions are often made of partly recognizable words combined with indecipherable magic formulae and signs. For inscribed magic amulets with Egyptian or Egyptianizing deities see M. Whiting in *Cambridge*, pp.218–20 and references given below; (cf. also **53**). This example is unusually complicated and so is discussed at length although its true interpretation remains obscure.

Obverse (i): The iconography is unusual; there are no other examples to my knowledge of a serpent with a janiform head and identification is very uncertain. Youthful beardless janiform heads (usually laureate) are common on Roman Republican coins of the last decades of the 3rd century BC but have been variously identified as Janus, his son Fontus, the Penates, Romulus and Remus or the Dioscuri. There is also a later janiform head of Pompey on a coin of about 45 BC. (Although it is doubtful that the janiform heads on coins represent the Dioscuri, this identification might have been fitting here as the Dioscuri appear to have a connection with the Agathodaimon – see *LIMC* iii, 'Dioskouroi', no.246; and J.E. Harrison, *Themis: a Study of the Social Origins of Greek Religion* (1912) pp.304–5.)

The heads on the amulet, however, do look more female than male. Female janiform heads appear on 6th century BC Greek coins but a later example on an unusual Roman Republican coin of the 3rd century BC has been identified as Persephone (see below). Although these coins are much earlier than the amulet, it is possible that one of these types might have inspired this janiform head even if the engraver was unaware of its original identity.

If the head on the amulet is female, Isis could be intended; her head-dress is sometimes cursorily shown as three strokes like this (cf. *Mira et Magica* no.74c,d) and probably represents her lotus diadem. In this case there could be a connection with Isis-Thermouthis (*op.cit.*, no.74a,b) although she is usually shown with a human head or bust on a cobra's body rather than on an ordinary serpent's body. (The snake was the harvest goddess, Renenoutet or Thermouthis (Agathe Tyche), who in Greco-Roman times became closely syncretized with Isis.) Her counterpart was Serapis-Agathodaimon who had the serpent body of Agathos Daimon and head of Serapis. Both were protective gods who governed men's destiny and were divinites of life and death. They are often depicted on terracottas, coins etc. (e.g. *LIMC* v, 'Isis-Thermouthis', no.349 – a 1stc. AD Alexandrian coin, and no.358 (*Munich* iii, no.2663) – 2nd–3rdc. AD heliotrope gem showing both deities; Delatte/Derchain, no.223 – Serapis-Agathodaimon).

In Egypt, Isis and Isis-Demeter were closely identified but had separate cults. The two goddesses are often difficult to distinguish from each other as their attributes were interchangeable. However, they are sometimes shown side-by-side – evidence that they were not completely syncretized: Demeter was felt to be Greek while Isis even in her agrarian role kept her Egyptian character. It has been suggested that there was also some interaction between Isis-Thermouthis and Demeter, who may also have taken on the form of a serpent (see F. Dunand, *Le culte d'Isis dans le bassin oriental de la Méditerranée* i EPRO (1973) pp.86–8,91–2, n.1; and G. Dattari, *Numi Augg. Alexandrini* (Cairo, 1901) pl.11.845 – Demeter(?) with serpent body on a coin of Trajan). Could the janiform head reflect the co-existence in serpent form of the two goddesses who fulfilled the same functions but had separate cults?

On magical amulets Persephone (Kore) seems sometimes to have been absorbed by Isis (Bonner, *SMA*, p.40) and there may be some connection here. A female janiform head wearing a wreath of corn has been identified as Persephone (daughter of Zeus and Demeter) on a Roman Campanian coin, probably issued by the Carthaginians about 216–211 BC (H.A. Grueber, *Coins of the Roman Republic in the British Museum* (1910) 2, p.139, nos.145–50, pl.75.14). Persephone, as the daughter of Zeus and Demeter, could also be regarded as the daughter (in serpent form) of Serapis-Agathodaimon and Isis-Thermouthis (cf. J.E. Harrison, *op.cit.*, p.278). Persephone was supposed to have presided over the death of mankind; she had to spend six months of the year in Hades as wife of Pluto and six months on earth with her mother, Demeter.

Other serpent-bodied gods appear on gnostic gems: compare for example lion-headed Chnoubis amulets (Delatte/Derchain, p.54ff.) but there is no inscription or symbol to link the Exeter amulet with Chnoubis. A human-headed type of Chnoubis snake is also known and the third decan of Cancer is described as having a bust resting on a base with two female heads turned in opposite directions, though one wears a head-dress and the other a diadem (see Bonner, *SMA*, pp.54–5, n.18 *op.cit.*).

The obverse (i) inscription reads:

'NEIKH' could stand for NIKA (Νικα = victory – perhaps over death; cf. Delatte/Derchain, nos.124,199) or more likely could form part of the word ΝΕΙΚΑΡΟΠΛΗΖ (Νι(νει)κα(χα)ροπλης) which has solar connections and seems to be a generalized word of power. The stars on both sides of the gem would reinforce the solar significance; and janiform heads probably also have a solar nature (see R. Pettazzoni, 'Per l'iconografia di Giano', *Studi Etruschi* 24 (1955–6) pp.89–90).

ΝΕΙΚΑΡΟΠΛΗΖ (or ΝΕΙΧΑΡΟΠΛΗΖ) appears on a number of magic gems (Bonner, *SMA*, p.201) including two magnetite amulets where the motifs appear related to each other as well as to the Exeter amulet:

*Thorvaldsen*, no.1870 – ringstone, obv.: Anubis stands wrapped in a mantle holding a palm over his shoulder; rev. ΝΕΙΧΑΡΟΠΛΗΖ

*Mira et Magica*, no.38 – 2ndc. AD ringstone (F.1); obv.: ΝΕΙΧΑΡΟΠΛΗΖ is inscribed round a Medusa head; rev.: Mercury; he is assimilated to Anubis and plays a similar role as *psychopompus*. (Hermanubis (**41** here) is a fusion of the two gods.)

Reverse (ii): Anubis, in anthropomorphic form, is common on magic gems in his two rôles as *psychopompus* (conveyor of souls) and embalmer, as well as attendant of Isis. However, he is usually shown holding various attributes and wearing a military skirt or sometimes a long garment (see Delatte/Derchain, p.89ff.; Bonner, *SMA*, no.36ff.; *Cambridge*, no.512; *LIMC* i, p.862ff.).

On the Exeter gem Anubis, with a small animal tail and back paws, appears to be unclothed (cf. Delatte/Derchain, no.117). Although the diagonal grooves of his coat could possibly represent the long garment worn by Isiac priests, elsewhere the treatment of the folds and hem make drapery unmistakable (cf. Delatte/Derchain, nos.119, 125; Bonner, *SMA*, nos.43–4; *LIMC* i, p.862ff.). Here Anubis stands with forearms raised in the attitude of adoration more usual for the baboon (*cynocephalus*), the solar animal who worships either the rising sun or sometimes Horus/Harpocrates – but, unlike Anubis, the baboon is ithyphallic and has a long tail (see Bonner, *SMA*, pp.154–5, nos.245–7; Delatte/ Derchain, p.151ff., nos.198–200; *Cambridge*, no.505).

Although the Exeter amulet shows Anubis in the attitude of the *cynocephalus*, on several other gems the characteristics of the two deities appear confused and identification is less certain. Compare:

*Mira et Magica*, no.149 – 2nd–3rdc. AD cornelian (F.1); the *cynocephalus* (and snake) with phallus and tail but his head is more like a jackal's; his coat, apparently indicated by diagonal parallel lines, looks like a thick garment wrapped round him (recalling the mummified Anubis, see *Cambridge*, no.493).

*Munich* iii, no.2899 – 2nd–3rdc. AD yellow jasper; a jackal very similar to the Exeter Anubis (but with a baboon's long tail) stands in attitude of adoration; he has the same legs and his coat is also shown as diagonal grooves; on his head a snake and crown.

The inscription on the reverse (ii) reads:

If the initial vertical stroke stands for 'Φ', part of the inscription can be read as ΦΑΡΜΑΚΕ(Ι)Α (φαρμακεα) = poisoning/ poisons, spells, or witchcraft (cf. K. Preisendanz, *Papyri Graecae Magicae* (1928–31) 2, p.182).

In the field behind Anubis is a vertical dash above a star, and in front of him:

Round the bevelled edge (iii) are the letters and signs:

(iii)                                              3:1

This amulet is probably open to many interpretations but, besides its general solar significance, perhaps the most obvious is the theme of death and resurrection or rebirth.

2nd–3rd century AD

**55**   30/1993. SA1
From Tiverton Roman Fort (excavations 1981–6)

**Ringstone** (F.1), cornelian; stained with iron corrosion and broken in half.
12 × 9 × 1.5mm
Mount: iron ring, w.27mm, corroded; plano-convex hoop; broken and incomplete. (As *Britain*, fig.1, ring type III.)

Publ.: M. Henig 'Intaglii', in Valerie A. Maxfield, 'Tiverton Roman Fort (Bolham); Excavations 1981–1986', pp.77–8, pl.7, fig.25 *Proc. Devon Archaeol. Soc.* 49 (1991)

*Apollo*, nude, standing facing to the left with his *chlamys* over his left arm which rests on a pillar; behind him is his sacred tripod; in his left hand he holds a laurel branch.

**55**                                            4:1

4:1

Iron rings like this and **56–7** were forged and then the stones fitted by hand. The metal could be lipped over the edge to hold them in place. This stone probably became cracked and then broke as the iron expanded during corrosion.

This intaglio and **56–7,59** belong to Henig's distinctive Flavian group, ca.AD 70–120 (see M. Henig, 'The Chronology of Roman Engraved Gemstones', *JRA* 1 (1988) esp.pp.147–8). Stylistically it compares with Maaskant's 'Imperial Cap with rim style' also dated to the end of 1st–2nd century AD (*Hague*, p.302).

This Apollo type, which probably derived from a statue, is common on gems (with a number of variations) and is found all over the Empire, see:

*Aquileia*, no.61 – black jasper.
*Sa'd*, nos.55–6 – no.56, 1st to early 2ndc. AD cornelian (F.) is set in an iron ring similar to the ring from Tiverton.

End of 1st century AD

**56**    852/1989.1
Excavated in a context of AD 50–75 from the floor of the Roman *fabrica* in the fortress, Trichay Street, Exeter, in 1972–3

**Ringstone** (F.1), cornelian (light orange); in good condition but chipped at the back.
12.5 × 10 × 1.75mm
Mount: iron ring, only the bezel and a small part of the hoop (rounded in section) survive, max. diam.21mm. (As *Britain*, fig.1, ring type II.)

Publ.: M. Henig, 'The Chronology of Roman Engraved Gemstones', *JRA* 1 (1988) pp.147–8, fig.6; *idem*, 'Intaglios' in N. Holbrook & P.T. Bidwell, 'Roman Finds from Exeter', *Exeter Archaeol. Rep.* 4 (1991) pp.241–2, figs.104(1),105.

*Hermes/Mercury* standing as in **57**; on his left he holds his staff (*caduceus*) and has his cloak (*chlamys*) draped over his arm; he wears his winged hat (*petasos*) and holds his money bag out in his right hand. Groundline.

**56**    4:1

4:1

There are many gems in similar style:

*Britain*, no.41 (=M. Henig 'The Gemstones' in B. Cunliffe, *The Temple of Sulis Minerva at Bath* ii, *The Finds from the Sacred Spring*, pp.27–33, no.2) – cornelian (F.2)

*Hague*, no.822 – 1st–2ndc. AD flat cornelian in 'Imperial Round Head style'.

*Bari*, no.39 – 1st–2ndc. AD cornelian (F.1).

*Hanover*, no.1430 – slightly convex cornelian dated to 3rdc. AD.

*Kassel*, no.64 – yellow jasper dated to the 3rdc. AD; wings on his head.

*Dalmatian Gems*, no.58 – cornelian (F.1) dated 2nd–3rdc. AD; also App.6a.

Second half of 1st century AD

Apart from a few minor differences, this is stylistically very similar to **57** and can be dated to about the same period. Mercury's chin, mouth and nose are shown as three parallel strokes; his attributes are simplified and his cap is reduced to a small peak. (Compare also the fine 1st century AD example, **37**.)

Henig points out the importance of this gem set in its original ring ('Intaglios' *loc.cit.*) because it comes from a dated context. It supplies evidence for the dating of gems engraved in this widespread and distinctive 'Small Grooves style' to the late 1st or early 2nd century AD when classical forms were breaking down during the Flavian period. This dating is also supported by a number of sealings in almost identical style from the record office in Cyrene which was destroyed during Trajan's reign (AD 98–117) (see G. Maddoli, 'Le Cretule del Nomophylakion di Cirene' in *Annuario della Scuola Archeologica di Atene* 41–2 (1963–4) nos.68–93). The size, translucency and style of this gem are also comparable to examples from Bath dated to the second half of the 1st century AD (see *Britain*, no.41 below).

Mercury is common on gems from Britain, where his cult seems to have been particularly popular (*Britain*, nos.38–50). Limestone fragments belonging to a cult statue of Mercury (and other related objects) were found on the site of a Roman temple at Uley which probably dates from the 2nd century AD (see M. Henig *et al.*, 'Votive objects: images and inscriptions' in A. Woodward & P. Leach, *The Uley Shrines, Excavation of a ritual complex on West Hill, Uley, Gloucestershire: 1977–9*, English Heritage, Archaeol. Rep. 17 (1993) p.88ff., fig.76).

**57**   Ant.1278
Unearthed while sewers were being laid in Pennsylvania, Exeter, in 1873.

**Ringstone** (F.), heliotrope (bloodstone). 14 × 11mm
Mount: iron ring, incomplete, the flattish hoop missing below the shoulders, w.22mm from shoulder to shoulder (original external diam. ca.26mm). (As *Britain*, fig.1, ring type III.)

Publ.: M. Henig, 'A Roman Signet ring from Pennsylvania, Exeter', *Proc. Devon Archaeol. Soc.* 48 (1990), pp.185–6.

*Hermes/Mercury* standing as in **56** but wearing winged boots; and here his money bag has three projections (as in **37**). Groundline.

4:1

The iron setting is very roughly made and file marks have been left on the back of the bezel; on the right upper edge there remains part of the iron overlap which holds the stone in place.

This intaglio is very close stylistically to **56**; it is engraved in a similar cursory, simplified manner but Mercury's features, again shown by parallel strokes, are even more schematized; his money-bag has three projections rather than one and his winged boots are indicated by two horizontal grooves above his ankles. Other examples of heliotrope gems of about the same date come from Bath and Tiverton.

Besides **56** (and **37**), compare:

A. Hamburger, 'Gems from Caesarea Maritima', *'Atiqot* 9 (1968) no.23 – heliotrope.

Late 1st or early 2nd century AD

**57**                              4:1

**58**   274/1990.G16
From Seaton Roman villa (1978)

**Ringstone** (F.2) glass paste imitating nicolo; good condition with not much sign of wear.
11 × 8 × 2.5mm
Mount: fragment of bronze ring bezel. (Probably as *Britain*, fig.1, ring type VIII – 3rd century AD.)

Publ.: M. Henig, 'The Intaglio' in 'Excavations at Honeyditches Roman Villa, Seaton, in 1978', *Proc. Devon Archaeol. Soc.* 39 (1981) p.74, pl.3b.

A *Satyr*, nude, walking to the left with a staff – probably a throwing-stick (a *lagobolon* or *pedum*) – in his left hand and holding out a bunch of grapes in his right hand. A short groundline?

**58**                                    4:1

Henig points out the miniaturistic style and the crisp execution of this glass gem which suggests it was cast directly from a mould made from a slightly earlier cut stone (of the Classicizing style of the 1st or 2nd century AD) rather than from another moulded copy which was often the case in the 3rd century AD.

Satyrs are common subjects on gems (as well as other objects) and are often shown in this or a similar position, usually with a goat-skin (*nebris*) over the left arm (*Aquileia*, no.390ff. and pp.188–9). A number have been found in Britain (see below).

For similar examples, though sometimes without a *nebris*, see:

*Caerleon*, no.63 – nicolo (F.2) ca.AD 160–230; a naked satyr dances to the right with a goat-skin over his arm.
    no.64 – red jasper; here the satyr faces to the left as is more usual.
*Britain*, nos.159–77 – similar dancing or walking satyrs – some without a *nebris*; several in nicolo or nicolo paste; pp.206–8.
*Aquileia*, no.393 – cornelian.
*Göttingen*, no.325 – 2ndc. AD nicolo; a different style.
*Germania* 56, p.494, no.20 – 2ndc. AD nicolo.
*Nijmegen*, no.133 – 3rdc. AD glass paste imitating nicolo.

3rd century AD

**59**   30/1993.SA2
From Tiverton Roman Fort (excavations 1981–6)

**Ringstone** (F.1), heliotrope (bloodstone); good condition but some chipping on the sides and abrasion on the upper surface. 12 × 10 × 1.5mm

Publ.: M. Henig, 'Intaglii' in Valerie A. Maxfield, 'Tiverton Roman Fort (Bolham): Excavations 1981–1986' pp.77–8, pl.7, fig.25, *Proc. Devon Archaeol. Soc.* 49 (1991); *idem*, 'The Bath Gem-Workshop: Further Discoveries', *Oxford Jnl. Archaeol.* 11 (2) (1992), pp.241–3; M. Henig, *The Art of Roman Britain* (1995) p.81, ill.48a.

*A Horse* in profile to the right with its head lowered as if grazing. Groundline.

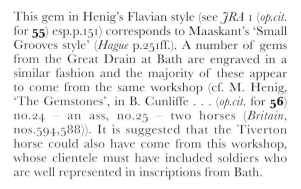

This gem in Henig's Flavian style (see *JRA* 1 (*op.cit.* for **55**) esp.p.151) corresponds to Maaskant's 'Small Grooves style' (*Hague* p.251ff.). A number of gems from the Great Drain at Bath are engraved in a similar fashion and the majority of these appear to come from the same workshop (cf. M. Henig, 'The Gemstones', in B. Cunliffe . . . (*op.cit.* for **56**) no.24 – an ass, no.25 – two horses (*Britain*, nos.594,588)). It is suggested that the Tiverton horse could also have come from this workshop, whose clientele must have included soldiers who are well represented in inscriptions from Bath.

This is a common subject and there are a number of gems in similar style:

*Naples* 1, no.260 – jasper.
*Merz*, no.225 – 1stc. BC onyx.
*Vienna* 1, nos.376–8 – but these are dated rather earlier, to the 1stc. BC.

End of 1st–early 2nd century AD

**59**                              4:1

**60** 852/1989.2
From Trichay Street, Exeter (excavations 1972–3)

**Ringstone** (F.), light green glass.
13 × 11mm
Mount: bronze ring, with a heavy hoop having a central ridge and rising to pronounced triangular shoulders; ht.23 × w.27mm. (As *Britain*, fig.1, ring type VIII – 3rdc. AD.)

Publ.: M. Henig, 'Intaglios' in N. Holbrook & P.T. Bidwell, 'Roman Finds from Exeter', *Exeter Archaeol. Rep.* 4 (1991) pp.241–2, figs.104(2),106.

4:1

*A Simplified figure* standing with arms stretched out sideways; the left arm resting on a staff. Groundline.

A number of moulded glass intagli with debased, stick-like figures and other simple motifs have been found in Britain – mostly in the south – see *Britain*, pp.132–3, distribution map fig.2, and no.539ff. They are often set in bronze rings which approximate to the normal 3rd century AD shape (see also **61** and *LondonRings*, no.1402). These are 3rd century AD 'Romano-British imitations' and Henig points out how they illustrate the downward movement of Romanizing ways (including the use of seals) to the lower orders of Roman society.

Henig has divided the motifs on the intagli into six types. For other examples of type 2, see:

*Britain*, nos.549–51 – from Uley, Cirencester and Hamstead Marshall.

3rd century AD

**60**                    4:1

**61**   852/1989.3
From Trichay Street, Exeter (excavations 1972–3)

**Ringstone** (F.), light green glass, lower left edge chipped.
diam. 7mm
Mount: bronze ring with most of the hoop now missing; a triangle is engraved on the hoop at either side of the raised bezel (original external diam. ca.18mm). (As *Britain*, fig.1, ring type VIII – 3rdc. AD.)

Publ.: M. Henig, *Exeter Archaeol. Rep.* 4, *op.cit.* for **60**, pp.241–2, figs.104(3),107.

A *Simplified two-pronged figure* shown as three blobs.

4:1

This ring with its glass intaglio belongs to the same group of Romano-British imitations as **60** described above, but the motif here is even more simplified and belongs to type 5.

For another example of figure type 5, see:

*Britain*, pl.30, App.164 – black paste intaglio with fragmented design perhaps representing a human figure; in ring type VIIIa – 3rdc. AD. From Upmarden, Sussex.

3rd century AD

**61**                4:1

## ROMAN LEAD SEALINGS: (**62–5**)

Lead sealings with impressed inscriptions and other motifs have been found in large numbers in Britain, France and elsewhere. There are many types of lead sealings, both private and official, and they were used for a variety of purposes. Similar sealings which have been found in widely separated parts of the empire can help throw light on ancient trade routes and the movement of goods (M.C.W. Still, 'Parallels for the Roman Lead Sealing from Smyrna found at Ickham, Kent', *Archaeologia Cantiana*, 114 (1994), pp.347–56).

Small objects such as writing tablets could have been secured by a wax sealing in a seal-box, but lead sealings (which often retain the impression of, or hole for, a cord or wire) would have been attached to large bales of merchandise, official stores and packages. There has been much discussion about the uses of lead sealings and their method of attachment: some types could have been used actually to seal and secure the goods while others may have been 'labels which simply dangled from threads attached to packages' (M.C.W. Still, 'Opening up Imperial Lead Sealings', *JRA*, 6 (1993), pp.404–8; *RIB* 2 'Instrumentum Domesticum' . . . fasc.i (*RIB* 2401–2411); . . . Lead Sealings, pp.87–8).

The majority of lead sealings found in Britain are official, though there are a few private ones. For most lead sealings special dies seem to have been used but a few (e.g. **65**) appear to have been sealed with intagli from finger rings and perhaps belonged to private individuals.

Five lead sealings (**62–5** and one not located – Montague no.637, p.63 (*RIB* 2411.42)) were bought by Montague in February 1927 from G.F. Lawrence, a London dealer, and were said to have come from the (Baron) Nugent collection. S.E. Winbolt gives his interpretation of these sealings in a letter to Montague dated 7 March 1927. Although they were reported to have come 'from Syracuse' they are unlike sealings from there and correspond closely to some of the types found in the waste heap outside the Roman fort at Brough-under-Stainmore, Cumbria [Westmorland] on the road from York to Carlisle. Large numbers of discarded sealings were found at Brough, which appears to have been a collection point for goods from a wide region. The packages must have been opened at Brough and the goods re-distributed. It is uncertain what these packages contained but examples with the abbreviation for *metal(la)* show an association with the mines. It is generally accepted, because of the known location of certain units, that the Brough sealings date to the 3rd century AD (see Richmond, I.A. 'Roman leaden sealings from Brough-under-Stainmore', *Trans. Cumberland and Westmorland Antiquarian and Archaeol. Soc.*, vol.36 n.s. (1936) pp.104–25, p.114). The Montague sealings have now also been assigned to Brough (see *RIB* 2, fasc.i, p.117, *RIB* 2411.254).

**62** 5/1946.758 (Montague no.636, p.63)
Ex coll. Baron Nugent
Probably from Brough-under-Stainmore
(see pp.78, 132)

**Lead sealing**, impression on both sides;
the string hole not visible.
Overall: 23 × 17 × ca.7mm
Impressions: obv.19 × ca.8mm; rev.17 ×
ca.7mm

Publ.: *RIB* 2, fasc.i, 'Lead sealings:
Miscellaneous', p.117, *RIB* 2411.254; R.P.
Wright, 'A new leaden sealing from York, and
further examples from Brough-under-
Stainmore', *Trans. Cumberland and Westmorland
Antiquarian and Archaeol. Soc.* n.s.54 (1955)
pp.102–4.

Obverse: EQS cross crescent
Reverse: OFP cross

4:1

**62**

4:1

Obverse: The first letter has been read at
different times as E, I or C and various
interpretations have been given (*RIB, loc.cit.*).
Still has pointed out that the form the sealing
takes is typical of almost all military sealings:
the matrix for the obverse was a container with sides
into which the molten lead was poured and then
the matrix for the reverse was pushed into it,
forcing out some of the lead round the edges.
Sealings made in this way would therefore have
a large reverse with irregular edges and a
smaller obverse with very regular, shaped edges.
The container matrix for the obverse bore the
title of the unit and the ordinary stamp matrix
(for the reverse) the name of the man in
charge at a particular time. This would
mean that the container matrix could
have been used by different individuals
who could have then used their own seal
for the reverse. It is uncertain whether
the moulds for the obverse of these
sealings were made from metal or fired
clay; none has been found so far – perhaps
because they were destroyed to prevent
unauthorized use. As the Exeter sealing was
made in a container matrix it is almost certainly
military; for this reason Still believes that the
most likely reading for the obverse is EQS and
so the sealing would belong with those of the
'Equites Singulares (consularis)', the governor's
mounted bodyguard, (cf. *RIB, op.cit.*, p.102,
2411.91 from Catterick; and *Britannia* 22 (1991),
p.298, no.14 from Carlisle).

Reverse: The letters OFP may stand for the *tria
nomina* of a private individual, though the O is
unusual and Q might have been expected. On the
other hand the letters might have a military
significance.

3rd century AD

**63**   5/1946.760 (Montague no.638, p.63)
Ex coll. Baron Nugent
Probably from Brough-under-Stainmore
(see pp. 78, 132)

**Lead sealing**, impression on both sides;
fractured; the string hole runs vertically.
Overall: 20 × ca.16 × ca.4–5mm
Impression: obv. ca.16 × 12mm; rev. 17 ×
ca.12mm

Publ.: *RIB* 2, fasc.i, 'Lead sealings: Cohorts'
pp.114–15, *RIB* 2411.232; R.P. Wright, *loc.cit.* for **62**

Obverse:   crescent | *c(ohortis)* $\overline{VII}$ *T(hracum)* |
            palm branch
Reverse:   T V D | star above crescent
            perhaps   *t(ut)ud(it)*, 'struck (*or*
            stamped) (this)'

4:1

The largest group of sealings found at Brough
(i.e. about 50) bears the abbreviation for *Cohors
VII Thracum*. Different products were handled at
Brough, mostly from three different areas. It is
uncertain what these packages contained but
some sealings with the abbreviation for *metal(la)*
show an association with the mines. (The
drawing in *RIB*, *loc.cit.*, does not show the
crescent beneath the star on the reverse of this
sealing.)

3rd century AD

**63**                                              4:1

**64**   5/1946.761 (Montague no.639, p.63)
Ex coll. Baron Nugent
Probably from Brough-under-Stainmore
(see pp.78, 132)

**Lead sealing**, impression on both sides; the obverse damaged; the string hole runs vertically.
Overall: 19 × ca.16–18 × ca.4–5mm
Impression: obv. ca.17 × ca.14mm; rev. ca.16 × ca.12mm

Publ.: *RIB* 2, fasc.i, 'Lead sealings: Cohorts' pp.114–15, *RIB* 2411.233; R.P. Wright, *loc.cit.* for **62**

This sealing appears to be the same as **63** although the obverse is very indistinct.

4:1

3rd century AD

**64**                              4:1

**65**   5/1946.762 (Montague no.640, p.63)
Ex coll. Baron Nugent
Said to have been 'found at Syracuse' like
**62–4** (but probably from Brough-under-
Stainmore, see pp.78,132)

**Lead sealing**, impression on obverse;
reverse a blank, oval convex dome with signs
of string holes about halfway along near the
edge of the two longer sides.
Overall: 16 × ca.13 × 5mm
Impression: obv. 12 × 10mm

Publ.: R.P. Wright, *loc.cit.* for **62**; *Britain*,
no.822.

The motif on this lead sealing is very
indistinct and various suggestions have been
made for it:

'Two figures (male and female) facing
inwards, holding hands (perhaps dancing)' –
Montague, no.640, p.63.

'. . . two figures of which the left, facing
right, kneels in supplication on right knee
and holds up both hands, while the right
figure facing left, bends down and extends
the left arm in clemency' – R.P. Wright
(*loc.cit.*); see also *Britain*, no.822.

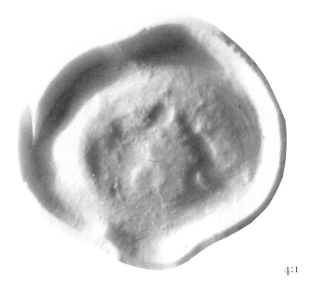

4:1

The impression on this lead sealing was probably
made with the signet-ring of a private individual.
Although the lead sealing itself may date, like the
others here (**62–4**), to the 3rd century AD, the
ring and/or ringstone could well have been rather
older. The sealing was bought with **62–4** which
probably come from Brough-under-Stainmore, but
no other examples of this two figure motif
are recorded (or identifiable) from there.
However, a number of other private sealings
(perhaps of the commandant) have been found at
Brough – for example the contest between Pan
and a goat (*Britain*, no.811; BM – 74,12–28.80).

The figures could be confronting cupids who
often are shown engaging in various pursuits on
gems and other objects – see for example the jet
pendant from Colchester (M. Henig, *The Art of
Roman Britain* (1995) p.135, fig.83 (BM
1852.6–26.1)). The motif, however, perhaps most
resembles the very popular scene of two cupids
wrestling. Compare, for example:

*Hague*, nos.387–8 – dated end 1stc. BC–beginning
of 1stc. AD; see literature.

3rd century AD or earlier

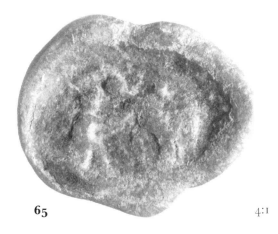

**65**                              4:1

# III  SASSANIAN SEALS AND A BACTRIAN RINGSTONE: (66–82 & 83)

The Sassanian Empire of Persia in the Levant lasted from AD 224 to 651. During the preceding Parthian period (about 211 BC–AD 224) there had been a strong Greco-Roman influence in Iran, but the Parthians do not seem to have had a glyptic tradition of their own and they imported gems from the west. The Sassanians, however, did produce their own seals and developed a distinctive style. Although there was an overlap of about a hundred years with the late Roman period, Roman influence is slight.

Some Sassanian seals can be dated to the end of the 3rd century AD but most are ascribed to the 4th–6th centuries AD. Not many actual seals have turned up in excavations although quite a number of clay bullae have been found. Historical figures depicted on seals, inscriptions (often personal names or titles) and seal shapes help to date Sassanian seals. A broad chronology of seal shapes has been suggested by A.D.H. Bivar (*LondonSass*, pp.23–4). Ringstones which reflect Roman shapes (**66,70,72,75,79**) are probably slightly earlier than the more common stamp seals which have perforations for suspension. There are also rings made entirely of stone or metal (see the unusual brass ring **82**). The stones most commonly used are once again varieties of quartz (cornelian, chalcedony, banded agates and jaspers) as well as haematite (see Appendix Ia and Ib, pp.135–6). Certain stones seem to have been more popular at some periods than others.

The repertoire of motifs is fairly limited and conventional subjects are frequently reproduced in an almost identical manner. There are portraits, animals (sometimes of astrological significance), fantastic animals, and devices (*nišan*). Engraving is frequently rather cursory and stylized with very obvious use of the cutting wheel. The round drill is used to hollow out smooth globular forms and details are added with wheel grooves which usually show little variation in width.

Except for the ring (**82**) the Sassanian seals in the Exeter collection belong to the standard repertoire. The inscribed Bactrian ringstone (**83**), however, is especially interesting and unusual.

See especially, A.D.H. Bivar, *Catalogue of Western Asiatic Seals in the British Museum. Stamp Seals II, the Sassanian Dynasty* (1969) (abbr. *LondonSass*); C.J. Brunner, *Sasanian Stamp Seals in the Metropolitan Museum of Art, New York* (1978) (abbr. *N.Y.Sas*); R. Gyselen, *Catalogue des sceaux, camées et bulles sassanides de la Bibliothèque Nationale et du Musée du Louvre*, 1. Collection Génerale (1994), 2. P. Gignoux, Les sceaux et bulles inscrits (1978) (abbr. *BN/LouvreSass* 1, 2); M. Henig, *Classical Gems: Ancient and Modern Intaglios and Cameos in the Fitzwilliam Museum, Cambridge* (1994) (abbr. *Cambridge*).

**66**   86/1966 (Corkill, M.9)
From Tello(?)

**Ringstone** (B.3 – *LondonSass* Bezel B),
cornelian.
13 × 10 × 5mm

*Draped bust of a man* in profile to the right,
with a pointed beard and straight hair bound
round his head; plant border above.

**66**                                    4:1

as private individuals who can sometimes be
identified by inscriptions and the insignia of
office (*QAN*, p.68ff.). Compare the 'Scratch style'
bust **67**.

For similar portraits see:

*N.Y.Sas*, p.57, no.47 – early 5thc. AD chalcedony
    ellipsoid (style B); with inscription above.
*Vienna 3*, no.2295 – slightly convex ringstone (B.3);
    similar but less cursory and with inscription.
*Geneva 1*, no.103 (=Göbl 7a¹⁴) – end 4th–beginning
    5thc. AD cornelian stamp seal.
Von der Osten, H.H., *Ancient Oriental Seals in the
    Collection of Mr Edward T. Newell* (1934) pl.35,
    no.620 – mottled jasper ellipsoid; wreath border.
Borisov & Lukonin, no.66 – same type, with rope
    border; also nos.31,70 – with inscriptions.
*BN/LouvreSass* 1, 20.D.1 – 3-layered convex onyx
    ringstone; similar hair style and with earring
    but less cursory; Parthian inscription and one
    Bactrian word.
    20.D.36 – agate ellipsoid; cursory portrait with
    the same plant border above.
    20.D.37 – layered white agate stamp seal;
    Pahlavi inscription.

3rd–4th century AD

A cursory gem with details of hair and garment
shown by straight wheel grooves. Convention-
alized male portraits of this type are common on
Sassanian seals (*LondonSass*, AC 1ff.). They
represent kings, nobles, officials, and magi as well

**67**  5/1946.377 (Montague no.236d, p.21A)
From Clements (8s 6d) 1917 (see p.131)

**Stamp seal** (ellipsoid), chalcedony (darkish
brown); polished surface with very few chips.
ht.21 × w.26/18mm; (perforation: diam.6mm)
Intaglio face: 20 × 16mm

*Draped bust of a bearded man* in profile to the
right; his straight hair is bound with a fillet
and in a bunch or loop behind; sprays of
foliage surround the head.

**67**                                              4:1

This is engraved in the cursory 'Scratch style' (see
examples below). Straight wheel grooves running
in different directions form a pattern of lines;
drapery is shown by horizontal folds on his
shoulders and vertical folds on his chest. For a less
schematic version of this hair style see *LondonSass*,
AC 22. See remarks for **66**.

For similar portraits, compare:

*LondonSass*, AG 1–3 – 3rd–4thc. AD ellipsoids, two
   chalcedonies, one cornelian; busts in the
   schematic 'Scratch style'.
*Lewis*, no.274 – 3rd or 4thc. AD chalcedony
   ellipsoid; similar style; trifoliate plant in front.
*BN/LouvreSass* 1, 20.D.53 – sardonyx ellipsoid;
   similar, and with trifoliate plant behind.

3rd–4th century AD

**68**   5/1946.375 (Montague no.236b, p.21A)
From Clements (10s) 1917 (see p.131)

**Stamp seal** (cabouchon – but possibly a
dome re-used), chalcedony (yellowish
beige); unpolished, very slightly convex
back with deep chips; perforation.
ht.16 × diam.29mm

*Bust of a king* with a pointed beard and
his hair in three thick ringlets; he wears
a diadem, earring and necklace. A
flower; or a device(?) – a crescent on a
standard with two smaller crescents on
either side below. Inscription in
blundered Pahlavi:

**wl'n ZY ...**

4:1

**68**                                              4:1

The motif is engraved on the convex side with
smooth, broad grooves and details of hair,
beard, dress, etc. are added with straight,
narrow grooves.

There are signs of straight engraved lines
on the flat back of the seal but the motif –
perhaps a 'gayomard'? (cf. **69**) – is no longer
identifiable as the surface is worn and there
are large chips. It is possible that this is a re-
used dome-shaped stamp seal engraved at
some later stage on the convex side. (For the
shape, compare *Vienna* 3, no.2370 – also with
engraving on the convex side.)

It is uncertain whether this seal is genuine or a
fake. The inscription in blundered Pahlavi appears
to start with an attested name, **wl'n** followed by a
miswritten **ZY** but after that the characters are
too mis-shapen to make out. A.D.H. Bivar
suggests that it is the product of someone who did
not know Pahlavi trying to copy a correct Pahlavi
inscription – either an illiterate Sassanian Persian
or a modern gem-forger. There are several groups
of seals with similar male busts and such
barbarous inscriptions (see examples below).

For the name see: P. Gignoux, *Noms propres
sassanides en Moyen-Perse épigraphique* (Vienna: 1986),

p.172, no.932, p.173, no.939 and p.174, no.947 – Middle Persian renderings of the Parthian name Vardanes, written **wl'n**, **w'l'n**, and **w'lt'n** in Pahlavi. The name appears on other seals:

*LondonSass*, CG 14 – **wld'n** in first line of an inscription on the reverse of an ellipsoid translated by Henning (in a letter) as 'Redeem (imp. pl.) Vardanes!'

*Sotheby Sale Catalogue* 9 April 1891, lot 18 (no illus.) – 'An excellent carved Bead, with name and titles of Varanes, and floral device, *Chalcedony*'; no portrait bust is mentioned. From the collection of the Revd W.F. Short.

Compare:

*LondonSass*, ZA 1–3 – ringstones which seem to be 18th century copies of an original now come to light: ZS 1 – ringstone, Bezel C (C.3). (ZA 1–3 =Göbl, pl.37, nos.4–6, and cf. also nos.7–11.)

Göbl, pl.37, nos.8–10 (*Coll. de Clercq* 2 (1903) nos.118–20) – modern fakes.

*BN/LouvreSass* 2, pl.28, 9.48 – similar to the fakes above.

Problematic: Sassanian or modern?

**69**   5/1946.353 (Montague no.353, p.20)
Found in the River Euphrates

**Stamp  seal**  (slightly  oval  dome), chalcedony; large chips on the face and round the edge; corroded iron still in the perforation.
ht.20 × w.24/27mm
Intaglio face: 26 × 24mm (convex)

Publ.: *Bazaar*, 17/7/09, p.152, fig.23.

The  constellation  *Orion*  (or  so-called '*Gayomard*' figure) seen frontally with legs and arms outstretched holding a staff in either hand; a dog (or rat) at his feet.

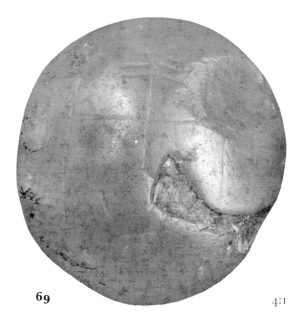

**69**                                                    4:1

This stone belongs to a large group of amulets with this schematic, stick-like figure engraved with simple straight lines. Many examples of this motif are engraved on conoid shaped stones with only slight variations in the figures and attributes.

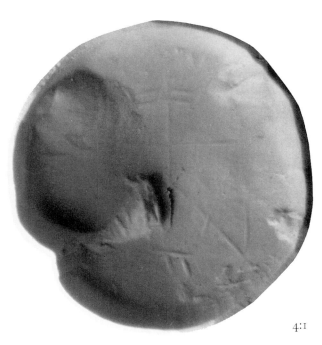

4:1

The figure is quasi-human with a nude, hairy body and shaggy hair. It most probably represents the constellation Orion with his dog as he appears on western star-maps rather than the primeval man or 'Gayomard'. Not all details are visible as the seal is chipped and worn; other examples sometimes show the figure with large ears, or ithyphallic and the staves with star markings (see *LondonSass*, pp.23,26; *N.Y.Sas*, pp.68–70 for descriptions and references to the 'Gayomard' in literature).

There are a number of close parallels:

*N.Y.Sas*, pp.70–1, no.156 (=*QAN*, p.38, pl.4.1) – chalcedony dome (Style D); very similar with the dog and star markings on the staves.
*LondonSass*, BF 1ff. (=Göbl 1b²) – less cursory examples.
  BF 8ff. – similar schematic examples.
*Hamburg*, no.96 – less schematic.
*Vienna* 3, no.2278 – with a rat.
*BN/LouvreSass* 1, 10.D.17 – agate stamp seal.
  10.D.18 – agate conoid; also 10.D.19–22 – agates and one chalcedony.

5th century AD or later

**70**   86/1966 (Corkill, M.7)
From Tello(?)

**Ringstone** (C.3, highly convex – *LondonSass* Bezel C), rock crystal; the surface appears rather worn.
10 × 8 × 5mm

A *lion seated or couchant* to the right with its head to the front.

**70**                                              4:1

A very cursory gem with little detailing. The lion, a symbol of strength, is the most common animal subject on Sassanian gems. It is uncertain whether it had an astrological significance in Zoroastrianism but it had a place in Roman Mithraic iconography. Many recumbent and striding lions with frontal faces were found on sealings at Qasr-i Abu Nasr. The nose and brow – often T-shaped – with turned up ends for ears is characteristic (*QAN*, pp.72–3). For the lion in Persian iconography see also *N.Y.Sas*, p.94ff.

For similar but less cursory examples, see:

*LondonSass*, DA 9–12 – 6thc. AD convex ringstones.
*N.Y.Sas*, p.97, no.16 – flat circular, nicolo ringstone
  (style B); 'sleeping lion' with crescent above (cf.
  **71** here); also nos.168,190 – domes.
*Cambridge*, no.912 – cornelian (F.4 – *LondonSass*
  Bezel D).

5th–6th century AD

**71**  86/1966 (Corkill, M.12)
From Tello(?)

**Stamp seal** (dome), iron; a large chip on the left side of the dome and small chips round the edge of the engraved surface.
ht.8 × w.9–11.5mm
Intaglio face: diam.ca.10mm

A *Lion*(?) *standing or walking* to the right with crescent moon above.

The engraving is cursory and the edge of the seal is chipped so part of the animal's head and front legs are missing. However, a lion (rather than a horse or zebu) is probably represented here as the animal appears to have a mane and its back legs end in lion's paws. Lions often appear with crescents.

For standing or walking lions in similar style or with a crescent moon, compare:

*LondonSass*, DC 1ff. – lions in cursory style, 5th
  and 6thc. AD;
  DA 5,6 – lions with crescents.
*Cambridge*, no.417 – 5thc. AD chalcedony
  dome; walking lion with crescent above –
  'perhaps a reference to the constellation
  Leo'.
*BN/LouvreSass* 1, 30.E.20 (=Göbl, 43c³) – metal
  stamp seal; very similar.
Borisov & Lukonin, no.306 – lion walking to the
  right with crescent above.

5th or 6th century AD

**71**  4:1

**72**   5/1946.380 (Montague no.236g, p.21a)
Ex coll. Prof. Churchill Babington; from
Clements, 1917 (see p.131)
Mentioned in a letter to Montague from
A.H. Smith 31/5/1917

**Ringstone** (F.4 – *LondonSass* Bezel D),
cornelian; slight wear on face, chip on right
edge.
11 × 10 × 2mm

*Winged horse* or *Pegasus* walking to the right;
one wing showing and harness; a bead
border.

**72**                                              4:1

very popular in Sassanian art and is most often
shown in this walking pose.

What are thought to be official sealings with
Pegasus and a Pahlavi inscription '**twly ZY
gšnsp** – Ādhur-gushnasp (or 'the Fire of the
Stallion') were found at Takht-i Sulaiman in
Azerbaijan on the site of the famous fire temple
where the sacred flame was thought to have
been brought down from heaven by a winged
horse (see Rudolf Naumann, *Die Ruinen von
Tacht-e Suleiman und Zendan-Suleiman*, Deutsches
Archäologisches Institut Abteilung Teheran.
Führer zu Archäologischen Plätzen in Iran,
Band 2 (1977), pp.70–1, Abb.49). Seals engraved
with this motif probably allude to this
legendary winged horse. But the winged horse
could represent the constellation Pegasus and
so also have an astrological significance (see
*LondonSass*, p.26; and for a discussion of the
single winged horse on various objects see
*N.Y.Sas*, p.82.)

For similar winged horses (but mostly on domes)
see:

*LondonSass*, ED 1ff. (ED 1 =Göbl, 70a³) – 4th–5thc.
   AD domes.
     EE 1 – 5thc. AD agate dome; similar style.
     EE 3,4,7 – 5thc. AD chalcedony, two cornelians;
     all bezel D (F.4) like the Exeter seal; the last
     two with bead borders.
*N.Y.Sas*, p.84, no.185 – a heliotrope dome (Style
     B); very similar. (Also pp.82–4, no.152ff.)
*Vienna* 3, nos.2403, 2406 – goethite and cornelian
     domes.
*Cambridge*, no.1011 – heliotrope dome; a good
     parallel. (Also nos.1007–10.)
J. Boardman & D. Scarisbrick, *The Ralph Harari
     Collection of Finger Rings*, no.104 – agate dome
     with inscription; same style.
*BN/LouvreSass* 1, 40.A.24 – layered agate stamp
     seal.

4th–5th century AD

Details are accurately engraved and this is close
to *N.Y.Sas*, Style B. The wing feathers are shown
by parallel grooves running diagonally above and
horizontally below. The two grooves on the chest
perhaps indicate a harness. The winged horse is

**73**  5/1946.722 (Montague no.577, p.57)
From Major Moore, 1919 (see p.132)

**Stamp seal** (dome), green jasper; later inscription on the dome.
ht.11 × widest diam.14mm
Intaglio face: diam.13mm.

*Hump-backed bull* (or *zebu*) sitting facing to the right.

Cufic inscription (retrograde) on the dome, ca.10th century AD:
'al-Ḥusain bin Yusuf, yathiq billah' – '(Seal of) al-Ḥusain, son of Yusuf, who trusts in God.'

4:1

**73**   4:1

The bull's body is smoothly rounded and details added with parallel horizontal lines which perhaps represent the rib-cage (close to *N.Y.Sas*, Style B).

In a letter to Montague, dated 5/4/1919 from the British Museum, J. Allan translated the inscription and suggested a date of about 'the 7th century AD – in any case not much later'. It has now been dated earlier.

This is a very common motif on gems – an indication of the importance of the bull in the Persian economy, mythology and religion. It might also, especially if accompanied by a star or crescent, stand for the sign of the zodiac, Taurus. For the bull, see *N.Y.Sas*, pp.77–8; *LondonSass*, p.26; Göbl, 53a.

Compare:

*LondonSass*, EN 1ff. – a number are very close in style to the Exeter example; EN 4,16 are both 5thc. AD green jasper domes.
EO 1–3.

*N.Y.Sas*, p.79, nos.24,33,20 – 4th–5thc. AD examples.

*Cambridge*, no.939 – 4thc. AD cornelian ringstone (F.1); very similar in style.

*Vienna* 3, nos.2358–9 – an ellipsoid and ringstone; both from Egypt.

*BN/LouvreSass* 1, 30.K.64 – green jasper stamp seal; also 30.K.65ff.

5th century AD

4:1

**74**   5/1946.719 (Montague no.574, p.56)
From Major Moore, 1919 (see p.132)

**Stamp seal** (dome), cornelian; chips on the dome.
h.10 × widest diam.14mm
Intaglio face: diam.12mm

*Stag* in profile to the right, recumbent and looking back ('lodged and regardant'); ribbons or diadem ties round its neck which float out in front; two beads on the right.

The stag is modelled with broad drill grooves without much fine detail (close to *N.Y.Sas*, Style B but rather simpler).

From prehistoric times stags appeared in Iranian art on all sorts of objects besides seals (e.g. on reliefs and silverware). They are shown either alone or sometimes as an eagle's prey or the quarry in hunting scenes. If the ribbons are diadem ties, the stag (like the ram, *N.Y.Sas*, pp.91–2) may have a royal connection; perhaps there was a royal hunting legend which is now lost. Stags seem to have had no mythological significance and so are shown naturally rather than winged (see *N.Y.Sas*, pp.87–90).

For stags in this position, besides **75**, see:

*LondonSass*, FA 5 – 5thc. AD green jasper dome. (Also FA 1ff.)

*N.Y.Sas*, p.90, no.188 – haematite dome; similar but simpler engraving (Style C); (also nos.88,129,79).

Göbl, +51a

**74**                                    4:1

5th century AD

**75**  86/1966 (Corkill, M.10)
From Tello(?)

**Ringstone** (F.1 – *LondonSass* Bezel D), cornelian; a chip on the top edge and on the right side.
ca.12–13 × 11 × 2mm

*Stag* 'lodged and regardant' as **74**, with a border of five beads.

**75**                                    4:1

This example is closer to *N.Y.Sas*, Style C; the engraving is more linear than **74** and the head is shown in outline.

For similar stags, besides **74**, see:

*Cambridge*, no.438 – 5thc. AD amethyst (F.1).

*LondonSass*, FA 7 – 5thc. AD goethite dome; stag in same style and position.
  FB 9 – 5thc. AD goethite ellipsoid; stag in similar style but not 'regardant'.
*BN/LouvreSass* 1, 30.J.46 – cornelian ringstone (F.1).

5th century AD

**76**  5/1946.720 (Montague no.575, p.57)
From Major Moore, 1919 (see p.132)

**Stamp seal** (dome), cornelian; slight chips on the dome.
ht.10 × w.12mm
Intaglio face: diam.12mm

*Long-horned ibex or wild goat* recumbent ('lodged') in profile to the right; a bead in the field in front.

**76**                                    4:1

The animal's body is shown by smooth rounded hollows and detailing is added with finer, narrow parallel grooves (cf. **73**). Its horns, legs and ear are engraved in rather thick, rounded wheel grooves. (Although the motif is very different, there is a marked similarity in the style of engraving to **81** which is said to have come from Egypt.)

Various long-horned animals appear on Sassanian seals and it is not always clear which types are intended (see *N.Y.Sas*, pp.99–101). Like Pegasus, goats and rams might possibly have had an astrological significance but this is uncertain.

For similar long-horned animals, see:

*Vienna* 3, no.2348 – 'antilope'; and no.2350 for style of engraving; both seals come from Egypt.

*N.Y.Sas*, p.100, no.150 (=Göbl, no.52a⁴, 'antilope (gazelle)') – meteoric iron ellipsoid (Style C); 'goat'.

*LondonSass*, FG 1–9 – 'ibex'; especially FG 3 & 9 – 5thc. AD goethite flattened dome, and a haematite dome.

    FG 1 – similar style.

*Cambridge*, no.431 – 5th–6thc. AD magnetite; 'ibex or long-horned goat'.

5th century AD

**77**    5/1946.721 (Montague no.576, p.57)
From Major Moore, 1919 (see p.132)

**Stamp seal** (dome), banded agate (greyish white/brown); good condition; some small chips.
ht.12 × w.15mm
Intaglio face: 11 × 12mm

*Two gazelles* (*antelopes*) sitting facing each other with their muzzles touching; a rope pattern arch above.

**77**            4:1

The animals are carefully engraved with broad rounded grooves – close to *N.Y.Sas*, Style B.

Although pairs of rams and stags are sometimes shown lodged and facing each other, gazelles seem to be more often shown side by side or standing (Göbl, 52f–q, 55e). The shape of the horns here is unusual and the artist must be attempting to portray a type of gazelle with horns which have a double curvature; they are usually shown with straight or slightly curved horns (cf. *LondonSass*, FH 1ff., FJ 1; Göbl, 52). For the rope pattern arch see *Geneva* 1, no.103 (=Göbl, 7a[14]).

Gazelles are popular in hunting scenes and are often shown on metalware: see *N.Y.Sas*, pp.100–1.

Compare:

*Corpus Inscriptionum Iranicarum*, pt.iii, vol.4 . . . *Sassanian Seals in the Collection of Mohsen Foroughi* (1971) R. Frye (ed.) pl.50.175 – chalcedony; a running gazelle with horns of the same shape.

*LondonSass*, ES 2 – 4thc. AD pink jasper, decorated ellipsoid; two rams lodged facing each other with a plant between.
  ES 4 – 5thc. AD cornelian ringstone; two rams as above.
  FF 1 (=Göbl, 51n) – 5thc. AD grey jasper dome; two standing stags, their muzzles touching; rather similar style.

*BN/LouvreSass* 1, 30.X.15 – agate stamp seal; two rams seated facing each other with their muzzles touching.

5th century AD  **78**

**78**  5/1946.376 (Montague no.236c, p.21A)
From Clements (10s) 1917 (see p.131)

**Stamp seal** (ellipsoid), chalcedony (darkish brown).
ht.22 × w.29/19; (perforation: diam.7mm)
Intaglio face: 22 × 17mm

*Two birds* with short necks, large heads and very short tails walking to the right; three short parallel strokes on the right of the field (water?), a crescent above and below, and a star on the left.

4:1

4:1

The birds are engraved with wide grooves and without much detailing (compare *N.Y.Sas*, Style C).

Birds are common on Sassanian seals and were a favourite subject in Zoroastrian iconography but it is unclear what birds are represented here. They resemble ducks but their beaks are not very duck-like and ducks are usually shown with webbed feet and have curled feathers on their backs. They could possibly be crows or pigeons; the three parallel lines possibly suggest water; the star and crescent usually suggest an astral setting but there are no birds in a constellation. For various birds, see *LondonSass*, pl.21ff.; *N.Y.Sas*, pp.111–12.

For similar birds see:

*N.Y.Sas*, p.112, no.105 (=Göbl, 36a³) – chalcedony ellipsoid; a crow – but this has a longer tail.
    p.111, no.110 – chalcedony ellipsoid; a pigeon.
*LondonSass*, HH 1 (=Göbl, 36b) – 4thc. AD chalcedony ellipsoid; two birds facing with one looking back; a star above on the left; crows?
*Vienna* 3, nos.2322–4 – 'ducks'; from Egypt.

4th–5th century AD

**79**    86/1966 (Corkill, M.8)
From Tello(?)

**Ringstone** (A.3 – *LondonSass* Bezel B), garnet (var. almandine). (Tested.)
diam.9mm

*Pomegranate* plant with three flowers growing from two tri-lobed scrolling leaves below (or winged pedestal?).

4:1

A crisply engraved gem. Red garnets (H = 6–7.5), which vary in colour, fall into the almandine group and were often used for gems of this shape (see *LondonSass*, pp.35–6 for their sources). This motif probably represents a pomegranate – though it closely resembles the tulips (*N.Y.Sas*, pp.116–17). The pomegranate appears on various objects in Persian art as a decorative motif and also a symbol of fertility (*N.Y.Sas*, p.118; *QAN*, pp.80–1).

For the same motif engraved in similar style, see:

*LondonSass*, LA 6 – 5thc. AD garnet (var.almandine), also shape A.3; (cf. also LA 7ff.; LA 7=Göbl, 95d¹).
*Cambridge*, no.1023 – 5thc. AD dome with the same motif.
*Vienna* 3, no.2423 – cornelian; also shape A.3; from Egypt.
*QAN*, D.145 – a sealing with this motif and inscription above belonging to a priest of the Gushnasp fire (cf. **72** here).
*BN/LouvreSass* 1, 50.A.17 – sard stamp seal; three flowers with three petals on winged pedestal; very similar.

5th century AD

**79** (see also frontispiece)            4:1

**80**   5/1946.378 (Montague no.236e, p.21A)
Ex coll. Prof. Churchill Babington; from
Clements (6s) 1917 (see p.131)
Mentioned in a letter to Montague from
A.H. Smith 31/5/1917

**Stamp seal** (ellipsoid), chalcedony; chips on
the back and slight scratches on the face;
perforation off-centre.
ht.13 × w.15–9mm
Intaglio face: 10 × 7 mm

*Fire-holder* (or 'altar') with a single upper
plinth, three flames and two ribbons hanging
down obliquely underneath towards the base.

From stone fragments found at Pasargadae it has
been possible to reconstruct Zoroastrian fire-
holders. They stood about 112cm high on a square
pillar and had a three-stepped base and top. A bowl
was hollowed out on the top to hold a thick bed of
hot ash which would be needed to rekindle a wood
fire whenever necessary or to keep it burning
continuously if it were in a major temple. The fire
would probably have been used only for devotional
purposes. (For fire-holders see M. Boyce, *The History
of Zoroastrianism* (Leiden: 1982) pp.51–3.)

Three is the sacred Zoroastrian number and
the three flames here could have had a number of
significances – including perhaps the three sacred
fire establishments (*N.Y.Sas*, pp.119–21).

For similar fire-holders see:

*LondonSass*, LG 1–4 – 5thc. AD ellipsoids, agate,
chalcedony and two cornelians; LG 3 is very
similar but without the flames (LG 1,3 &
4=Göbl, 98a[4,7,8,]).
*Cambridge*, no.1041 – 5thc. AD ellipsoid,
chalcedony; with flames.
*BN/LouvreSass* 1, 60.2 – cornelian ellipsoid; no
flames. From Susa.

5th century AD

**80**                                    4:1

**81**   5/1946.357 (Montague no.220, p.20)
'Perhaps from Alexandria'

**Stamp seal** (dome), heliotrope (bloodstone);
small chips on the back and round the face.
ht.14mm × w.17
Intaglio face: diam.12mm

*Device* (Middle Persian '*nišan*') – a crescent on
a short standard over a chevron or forked
base with terminals; three beads in the field.

**81**                                          4:1

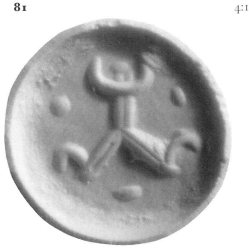

similar devices to this example (see *Vienna* 3,
nos.2431–3, 2435–8).

These personal or clan devices, which were
used to mark possessions or as insignia on
armour, may have developed from cattle-brands
used by the earlier nomadic Iranians. Members,
dependents and servants of a particular clan or
family probably used the same device. Some
examples include letters of the Pahlavi alphabet
and are probably monograms (see *LondonSass*,
p.28).

This simple device is related to a number of
quite common but more elaborate versions that
usually include a horizontal crossbar and
terminals (e.g. *LondonSass*, NH 5–6; *N.Y.Sas*,
pp.126–7, nos.202, 214); *Vienna* 3, no.2433 –
engraved also in similar style to this device).

For similar simple devices, compare:

*Vienna* 3, no.2432 – cornelian ellipsoid; similar but
   without the vertical shaft, engraved with
   double grooves; beads in the field. From Egypt.
*QAN*, D.17 – sealing; as *Vienna* 3, no.2432 above.
*LondonSass*, NG 1 – 5thc. AD goethite dome;
   vertical bar with broken crescent above, but
   with a straight horizontal, rather than forked,
   base; double grooves.
*Cambridge*, no.473 – 5th or 6thc. AD cornelian
   dome; vertical shaft with four crescents, and six
   beads in the field.

5th–6th century AD

The style of engraving with rather thick rounded
wheel grooves is similar to **76**. A number of
Sassanian seals come from Egypt – some with

**82** 5/1946.401 (Montague no.257, p.24)
(5s)

**Intaglio, brass ring**, cast; with punched and incised motif on a high projecting, slightly convex, cone-shaped bezel and two ridges on either shoulder. (XRF analysis.)
9 × 10 × ca.7mm
Ring: ht.29 (inc.bezel) × w.21mm; plano-convex hoop widening slightly towards the bezel.

Publ.: *Bazaar*, 14/12/07, pp.1707–8, fig.3

*Grotesque, bearded profile heads* or *masks* facing each other; a plant or arrow-head in the centre of the field above them and a border of dots.

2:1

**82**                                                              4:1

This ring is brass – a copper/zinc alloy. XRF analysis (undertaken by the Department of Materials, University of Oxford) shows that the bezel is an alloy containing 13.24% zinc and 86.44% copper. These proportions are very close to the average for Roman and later Islamic decorative metal (as well as for modern gilding metal). The lower part of the hoop, however, appears to be a later replacement because it contains 34.49% zinc and 64.89% copper; an alloy with such a high proportion of zinc could not have been produced by the cementation process used in antiquity (28% zinc was the maximum). (See P. Craddock, 'The Composition of the Copper Alloys used by the Greek, Etruscan and Roman Civilizations: 3. The Origins and Early Use of Brass', *Jnl. of Archaeological Science* (1978) 5, pp.1–16.) There are a few literary references to ancient Persian brass (see in H.E. Wulff, *The Traditional Crafts of Persia* (1966) p.12; P. Harper, *The Royal Hunter* (1978) p.87) but no actual examples appear to have been identified so far. If this ring is pre-Islamic it would be one of the first examples of Sassanian brass to be recognized, but the most plausible explanation may be that it is post-Sassanian work of non-Muslims following earlier traditions in the early Islamic period.

The earliest examples of similar ring-shapes with raised bezels are 5th century AD Sassanian (*LondonSass*, HB 6 – a bronze ring dated to the 7th century AD but this has a wider and lower bezel). The type is also found in Byzantine jewellery of the 6th century AD (see M.C. Ross, *Catalogue of the Byzantine and Early Medieval Antiquities in the Dumbarton Oaks Collection* 2 (1965) no.55 – 6th century AD bronze ring with monogram; nos.64–5 – 6th AD century gold marriage rings).

The shape continues from the 7th–9th century AD in early Islamic rings which often combine Byzantine and Sassanian features. Several examples cast in bronze with a punched motif correspond exactly in shape to the Exeter ring, see: M. Wenzel, 'Ornament and Amulet: Rings of the Islamic Lands', *The Nasser D. Khalili Collection of Islamic Art* 16 (1993) J. Raby (ed.) p.189, esp. nos.35,37,39; some have animal motifs derived from Sassanian models. The heads on the Exeter ring do not appear typically Sassanian – although they are so small that the details are ambiguous; nor is the iconography Islamic.

This ring is cast and the motif on the bezel is punched and perhaps incised. The small circular punch has been used, probably to represent hair rather than the studs on a helmet (cf. *LondonSass*, AA 4,5, AF 4; *Cambridge*, no.475 – a 3rd–4thc. AD Kushano-Sassanian ringstone); and the hair-roll is shown by small, parallel incised lines. The plant or arrow-like motif (Göbl, no.93a$^3$) between the heads appears quite often on Sassanian gems (e.g. *Lewis*, no.274 – in front of a bust; *LondonSass*, ES 2 – between two rams).

The heads without necks are perhaps inspired by the theatre masks which often appear on Roman gems; the features do show similarities with bearded grotesque or satyr masks which are sometimes shown with a hair-roll or wreath (cf. *F.Berlin*, nos.5227–8).

The caricature-like features are also reminiscent of the way Westerners are sometimes portrayed by Orientals: for example, the 7th century AD Tang funerary terracotta figure of a kneeling tributary wearing a fur-edged cap, M.-T. Bobot, *Musée Cernuski; promenade dans les collections chinoises* (1983), p.43 (M.C. 8971) or the terracotta heads of Iranian or Indo-Scythian men, J.M. Rosenfield, *The Dynastic Arts of the Kushans* (1967), fig.19.

This enigmatic ring appears to show a combination of influences and (except for the ring-shape) there is no close parallel. Compare:

G. Zahlhass, *Fingerringe und Gemmen, Sammlung Dr. E. Pressmar* (1985), no. 76 – Sassanian bronze ring from the Lebanon 5th–7thc. AD; a similar type of ring but with a pyramid-shaped bezel; a cursory Sassanian bearded bust in profile.

*Cambridge*, no.890 – stamp seal in the 'Scratch style'; a bearded head with no neck – 'copy of Western gem depicting a mask?'

*Getty*, no.324 – 1stc. AD Roman cornelian (F.1) mask with pedum; very similar to *Cambridge*, no.890 (above).

N.C. Debevoise, 'The Essential Characteristics of Parthian and Sasanian Glyptic Art', *Berytus* 1 (1934) pl.1.6 – also very similar to the *Cambridge* 'mask' and engraved in the same style.

*LondonSass*, BB 1 (=Göbl, no.17a), 4 – ca.4thc. AD ellipsoid and ringstone (Bezel E); male and female facing busts with inscriptions.

*Vienna* 3, no.2293 – Sassanian ringstone, bearded bust with similar hair style and profile; also the stamp seal, no.2297.

*BN/LouvreSass* 1, 22.1 – red jasper stamp seal; facing male busts.

Possibly Sassanian, 7th century AD
(or post-Sassanian, 7th–9th century AD?)

**83** 5/1946.374 (Montague no.236a, p.21A)
Ex coll. Prof. Churchill Babington; from
Clements (15s) 1917 (see p.131)
Mentioned in a letter to Montague from
A.H. Smith, 31/5/17

**Ringstone** (F.4), three layered sardonyx;
brown/white/translucent greyish-brown
chalcedony; irregular with slightly convex
face; surface scratched.
22 × 16 × 6mm

A *Horse* standing facing to the right; an object
in front of it (an altar, throne or symbol?) and
an inscription in Greco-Bactrian above.

Montague notes that this gem is 'possibly from
Persis' but the inscription identifies it as Bactrian.
(It has now been read by N. Sims-Williams.) The
use of seals was widespread in Central Asia
during the early centuries AD; some were made
locally and others imported. They took many
forms, were made in a variety of materials and
the quality of workmanship was very variable.
Their iconography and style of engraving show
Greek, Roman, Sassanian, Oriental and local
influences. For examples of these eclectic gems
see: Aurel Stein, *Serindia. Detailed Report of
Explorations in Central Asia and Westernmost China*
(1921) iv, pl.v – including walking animals on
layered agate; M. Maillard in *L'Asie Centrale*, L.
Hanbis (ed.) (Paris: 1977), pp.71–2, figs.40,

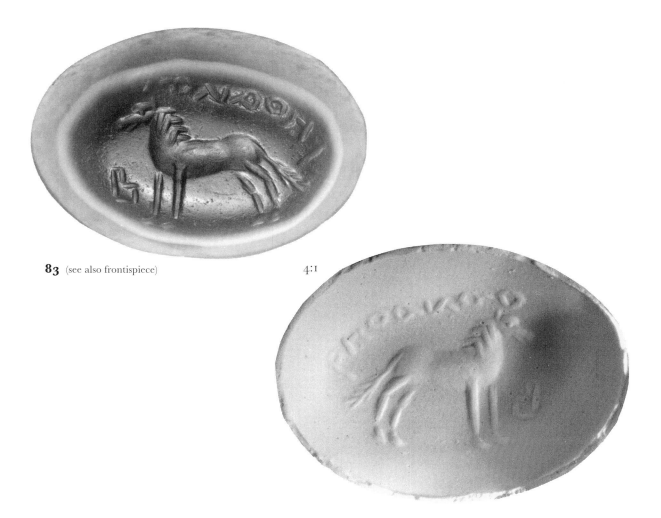

**83** (see also frontispiece)                    4:1

43,46,48; *Cambridge*, nos.475–89; J. Boardman in *The Crossroads of Asia; Transformations in Image and Symbol*, E. Errington & J. Cribb (eds.) (1992) nos.150–53 – three gems which rely closely on Greek designs.

Horses are very common on gems but this example seems unusual. It is unlike the typical plump Sassanian horse with rounded anatomy (cf. **72**) and seems more closely related to the leaner classical and Roman types (**59**). On Roman gems, though, single horses are more often shown galloping or with head down grazing (e.g. *Vienna* 1, nos.371–8; and **59** here). This animal, quite carefully engraved with wheel grooves, stands rather stiffly with its head up and back legs stretched out behind. The object in front of the horse is uncertain; it could be a symbol, a throne or perhaps an altar is most likely. Coins of the Bactrian king Hermaeus (ca.90–70 BC) have the bust of Zeus-Mithra on one side and a standing horse on the other. However, in India gold coins were issued by Samudragupta (AD 335–80) to be handed out to Brahmans on the occasion of the horse-sacrifice or Aśvamedha. On these coins a horse is shown standing before a sacrificial post (J. Allan, *BMC Gupta Dynasties* (1914) pp.lxxvi–vii, 21ff., pl.5.9ff.). Earlier lead coins of Sri Candra Satakarni (ca.AD 207–17) show a horse standing before a small hour-glass shaped object identified as an altar (E.J. Rapson, *BMC Andra Dynasty . . .* (1908) pp.32–3, pl.6.126ff.). (It has been suggested that the sacrificial horse was the sun horse.) If the object on the seal is an altar, the motif might also allude to horse-sacrifice though, to my knowledge, it does not seem to have been performed by the Kushans. However, they must have been aware of the practice (see J.M. Rosenfield, *The Dynastic Arts of the Kushans* (1967) p.115).

The inscription reads:

Although the letters of the inscription are unjoined, the letter-forms, especially the *d*, show the influence of the cursive variety of Greco-Bactrian script and can be read as *rēoando* – the Bactrian word for 'wealthy, rich'. (This is derived from the Old Iranian *\*raiwant-a-* and corresponds to Sanskrit *revánt-*, Avestan *raēuuaṇt-*, etc.) Adjectives with complimentary meanings were used for personal names and so this is probably the name of the owner of the gem. But it could also refer to the 'rich god' or 'rich (one)' who is often referred to in Sogdian personal names. This can be compared to the Bactrian personal name which is attested in unpublished documents: *bago-rē-marēgo* – 'servant of the rich god'. 'Bago' is the Bactrian form of 'Baga' and *ré* a short form of *rēoando*.) The god referred to in these names is probably Mithra, although his identity has been the subject of much discussion. The Sogdians did not actually use the name of Mithra for personal names but it seems they were familiar with the god and his name (see N. Sims-Williams, 'The Sogdian inscriptions of the Upper Indus: a preliminary report' in K. Jettmar *et al*. (ed.), *Antiquities of Northern Pakistan. Reports and Studies. 1. Rock Inscriptions of the Upper Indus Valley*, Mainz (1989) pp.135–6); *idem* 'Mithra the Baga' in P. Bernard & F. Grenet (eds.) *Histoire et cultes de l'Asie centrale préislamique*, Paris (1991) p.183).

A solar deity who often appears in Sogdian art in a horse-drawn chariot or on a throne supported by the foreparts of two horses has been plausibly identified with Mithra – but is never identified by name. Animals are often used to identify deities in Sogdian art and on a mural from Panjikent the small horse above a fighting warrior with a rayed nimbus seems to indicate Mithra (N. Sims-Williams, *op.cit*. (1991) p.178).

On this gem there could be an allusion to Mithra in both the inscription, *rēoando* ('the rich god'), and in the horse as a symbol of Mithra.

Bactrian, 2nd century AD or later

# IV   RENAISSANCE AND MODERN RINGSTONES: (84–6)

After the fall of the Roman empire the tradition of gem engraving never completely died out but has carried on in different parts of Europe to the present day. At the same time, ancient engraved gems have been found on Roman sites since antiquity, or have survived above ground (as highly prized objects) set into Byzantine and medieval jewellery, book covers, church plate and reliquaries. It was during the Renaissance, however, when large numbers of ancient gems (and coins) turned up in excavations in Italy, that they became eagerly sought after by collectors.

From the 15th or 16th century, ancient gems were used as models by gem engravers. Impressions in sulphur as well as illustrations of ancient gems in books were made for wide circulation so that the iconography could be closely copied, adapted or elaborated upon. From a mould it was possible to make an exact glass replica of an original – though sometimes the mould was slightly altered or 'improved' (see **86**).

Gems which copy the antique, more or less closely, can usually be recognized as modern – details are not always well understood (**84–5**) or the engraving (which is very often technically perfect) lacks the spontaneity of ancient models. However, it is not always easy to be sure whether a gem is ancient or modern and indeed some examples may be deliberate forgeries. (Many later gems, of course, portray contemporary figures or scenes.)

For a comprehensive range of modern gems, see D. Scarisbrick in M. Henig, *Classical Gems: Ancient and Modern Intaglios in the Fitzwilliam Museum, Cambridge* (1994) (abbr. *Cambridge*).

**84**  5/1946.717 (Montague no.572, p.56)
From William Green (see pp.131–2)

**Ringstone** (F.7), heliotrope (bloodstone) – a
mottled green jasper with red spots and light
ochre patches; slight scratching on surface;
slightly bevelled edge.
14 × 11 × 3mm

*Draped Bust of Bearded Emperor(?)* in profile to
the right with the ties of his laurel wreath
flying out behind.

**84** (see also frontispiece)                              4:1

widths but below his laurel wreath and on his
neck it falls in soft waves like his beard.

Montague doubted the antiquity of this gem
because 'bloodstone' or heliotrope was not often
used in the Roman period. Certainly, the head
bears little resemblance to ancient coin and gem
portraits of bearded Roman emperors and, as
with many modern gems, there is no hair shown
on his forehead below the laurel wreath. (Among
ancient gems, the head type is perhaps closest to
*Würzburg*, no.800 – a glass copy of an ancient
gem identified as Julian the Apostate (AD 360–3)
but again the usual fringe of hair frames the face.)

Although the Exeter gem appears of finer quality,
the closest parallels are:

*Bari*, no.100 – cornelian (also shape F.7) of
    'doubtful antiquity'; a very similar laureate
    bust with straight hair shown in parallel lines
    but a curly beard; see p.75.
*Cologne*, pl.137.10 – 'modern' octagonal gem; quite
    similar.
*Gaul*, no.500 – 1stc. BC? heliotrope (F.1); a
    beardless draped bust.

                    16th–18th century?

A finely engraved portrait with features carefully
outlined. The hair on the crown of his head is
engraved in narrow parallel lines of different

**85**  5/1946.710 (Montague no.565, p.56)
From William Green (see pp.131–2)

**Ringstone** (F.1), cornelian; shiny surface
and not much sign of wear.
13 × 9 × 3mm

*Draped bust of Mars/Ares(?)* or *Athena/Roma(?)*
in profile to the left with long hair and
wearing a close-fitting uncrested helmet with
a laurel wreath tied behind.

The face and neck are shown as smooth wide
grooves and details are carefully added with
narrow wheel grooves. The crown of the helmet
is shown by very narrow parallel grooves which
give the appearance of hair.

This gem must be modern as the helmet seems
to be misunderstood and does not correspond to
any ancient type; the laurel wreath or diadem
rather resembles a raised visor. It is uncertain
whether the bust is intended to represent
Ares/Mars or Athena/Roma.

Compare:

*Cambridge*, no.704 – 17th–18th century cornelian
    (F.7); head of Athena/Minerva 'wearing a
    helmet crowned with laurel' with ties behind
    (the ties and laurel misunderstood); a similar
    type but less well engraved.
*Bari*, no.97 – cornelian; bust of Athena/
    Minerva(?) of doubtful antiquity; features
    engraved in a similar way to the Exeter gem.
    no.123 – cornelian; male head of doubtful
    antiquity with diadem or *taenia*; hair on the crown
    of the head shown by very fine parallel lines.

18th century?

**85**                    4:1

**86**   5/1946.716 (Montague no.571, p.56)
From William Green (see pp.131–2)

**Ringstone** (F.4), glass imitating layered agate: reddish-brown/white/black. (Confirmed by SEM analysis.)
16 × 13 × 3mm overall
14 × 11mm intaglio face

A *Giant* has dropped on to his right knee to pick up a stone which he is about to hurl towards the right; his left leg is braced against a rock and he holds up a pair of spears in his left hand; his head, with pointed beard, is shown in profile to the right and he appears to wear a flat cap; his body is shown frontally, clad in a short belted *chiton* with an animal skin over his left shoulder and arm. A short groundline under his knee.

This gem is a glass copy which seems to have been moulded from an original Greek gem (**86x** here) in the British Museum (Payne Knight coll. no.1824/3-1/19=*London*, no.558; H.B. Walters, *Art of the Greeks* (1906) pl.91.19; *AG*, pl.10.48; Richter 1, no.309; *GGFR*, pl.538, pp.201,291). The original gem (shape F.1), a chalcedony or light golden sard (described as 'Indian onyx' by Payne Knight) measures 16 × 13 × 2mm; it appears to be a cut-down scaraboid with its edges trimmed and is dated about 400 BC – though Furtwängler (*AG* ii, p.53, no.48) describes it as a 'chalcedony ringstone'. SEM analysis of the Exeter glass copy shows it has a high potassium content and so it cannot be ancient; ancient glass was made with natron and usually has a high sodium content.

Minute details of anatomy and costume are very finely and carefully engraved and Walters in describing gems of this type says: 'the designs are extremely shallow, the lines fine and scratchy as in a delicate pen-and-ink sketch but these are points

**86x**                                                4:1

**86** (see also frontispiece)                        4:1

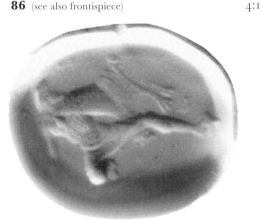

seen only under a magnifying glass'; he compares engraved designs of this type to those on gold rings of the period.

Kneeling and crouching figures had become popular on sculpture, vases, gems and coins from the early Classical period on (e.g. *GGFR*, pls.534,536, p.201). On this gem the giant's complicated position has been accurately drawn to give a feeling of perspective and depth – note especially the foreshortened right leg with the knee deeply engraved in the foreground and the small, shallowly engraved foot directly behind it. A kneeling, stone-throwing giant of similar type, though his body (but not his foot) is seen from behind, is illustrated on a red-figure vase of the early 4th century BC (see J. Boardman, *Athenian Red Figure Vases, the Classical Period; a Handbook* (1989) no.330).

Besides the colour and material, there are a number of differences between the original gem in London (**86x**) and the Exeter glass copy (**86**):

On the glass copy the surface appears rather worn, the image is shallower, and the fine engraved detail less clear – the spears, for example, are hardly visible. The glass copy or, more likely the mould for it, has been trimmed round the edge as the intaglio face is slightly smaller than on the original gem. Because of this, the stone which the giant is picking up and part of the rock against which he has his foot are missing. On the original there are large chips on either side of the giant's head which also appear on Payne Knight's pre-1824 sealing wax impression. As these chips do not appear on the copy, either the mould was made before the original was chipped or the mould was touched up. The groundline on the Exeter copy is no longer parallel with the longer side of the gem which makes the giant appear to be standing on one leg. This probably led Montague in his catalogue to describe the figure as 'rising from the ground'.

This subject seems unusual on gems, although there is another rather more summary version of a giant of this type on a scarab (the impression is in the Ashmolean Museum, Oxford – see *GGFR*, p.291). Other stone-throwing giants are shown as *anguipede* (e.g. *Vienna* 1, no.263 – 1st century BC; *London*, no.3098 – Augustan).

18th or 19th century glass paste copy
of a Greek original of about 400 BC

# V  AMULETS AND MISCELLANEOUS: (87–103)

For thousands of years amulets have been worn or carried for their prophylactic and apotropaic qualities – it was believed they would avert the evil eye, bring good luck and in many cases also help ensure fertility. Magic qualities were sometimes thought to exist in certain materials, as well as in the object itself or the image portrayed on it. Amulets, usually in the form of pendants, were worn as jewellery and so also had a decorative purpose. The motif and/or the material of a ringstone could also have an amuletic function, but most intagli also served as seals (cf. especially **47, 51–4**).

The same types of amulet, but often in different materials, continued for hundreds of years and are found over very wide areas (see for example the 'fica' hand (**90**)). As amulets were most probably treasured possessions and were sometimes handed down for generations, they are often very difficult to date precisely even when they come from recorded excavations as they could well have been hundreds of years old when they were buried.

A number of the amulets described here (**87–93**), as well as the pendant (**29**) had been bought at Glendining and Co. on 10 April 1913. They were said to have been brought in for sale together with ancient beads and other objects dating down to the Roman period by a 'Servian' who had been wounded in the war and who had acquired them at Tripoli in Syria (*Bazaar*, 2/7/13, p.8). The port of Tripoli was on the route from the interior and had been founded by the Phoenicians. Pompey freed it from a tyrant in the 1st century BC and it became the capital of a *conventus* of a Roman province. In the 3rd century AD it was used as a base for the Roman war fleet (see R. Stillwell and others, eds., *Princeton Encyclopedia of Classical Sites* (1976) p.935).

**87**   5/1946.372 (Montague no.235, p.21)
From Tripoli, Syria (see p.133)

**Scarab**, garnet (var. almandine); perforated
longitudinally; surface scratches and some
internal fractures. (Tested.)
14 × 10 × 8mm (plinth ht.5mm)

Publ.: *Bazaar*, 2/7/13, p.8, fig.11.

The wings, head and thorax of this scarab
are shown by simple engraved lines, the
plinth is plain without any indication of legs,
and the base uninscribed. This type of
simplified Egyptian scarab (sometimes even
the wings are not shown) can be dated to the
12th Dynasty (ca.1991–1786 BC) in the Middle
Kingdom period.

**87**                                                                 4:1

3:1

In Egypt scarabs were the most popular amulets.
They could be worn alone or strung on a cord
with other amulets or beads, set in necklaces and
from the 12th Dynasty made into swivel rings.
Scarabs were often inscribed on the base and so

could function as seals as well as amulets. In
Egypt the scarab, as a symbol of new life and
regeneration, was considered to be the most
powerful amulet – both for the living and for the
dead. They were worn by the living, but also
placed in burials. Most of the royal burials of the
12th Dynasty contained unmounted scarabs
which must have been worn on cords. From the
25th Dynasty and in the Late Period funerary
scarabs (sometimes quite large) were stitched on
to the mummy wrappings.

Scarabs were copied by local craftsmen in
Syria and Palestine, so this example could have
been imported or made locally. They illustrate the
Egyptian role there during the Middle Kingdom,
as well as the special relations between Egypt and
Byblos (see R. Giveon, *Egyptian Scarabs from
Western Asia from the Collections of the British Museum*
(1985) pp.15–16).

In Egypt scarabs are found in almost every
material known to the Egyptians, including
amethyst, garnet, turquoise, lapis lazuli, steatite
and composition. Garnets found in Aswan,
however, are small and were mostly used for
beads. But garnet became especially popular
during the Middle Kingdom – perhaps because at
that time minerals were being mined in Western
Sinai where larger specimens of garnet are found.
There are a number of 12th Dynasty garnet
scarabs. (See Aldred, *Jewels*, p.34 for garnet,
pp.60–1 for scarabs; Andrews, *Jewellery*, p.43 for
garnet, Andrews, *Amulets* (1994) pp.50–9 for
scarabs.)

For similar 12th Dynasty and later scarabs see:

J. Garstang, *El Arabah* (1901), Egyptian Research
Account 1900, Tomb E.30, pl.1, p.4 – a wrist
string of garnet beads, a plain garnet scarab,
a small glaze scarab and other glaze
pendants; another example in Tomb E.303,
p.6.
Andrews, *Jewellery*, p.164, pl.146f (EA 65316) –
plain amethyst amuletic scarab mounted in a
gold swivel ring from Abydos (ca.1820 BC).
pl.146g (EA 37308) – an obsidian example;
pp.177–8. (=Andrews, *Amulets* (1994) pl.45a & d).
Aldred, *Jewels*, pl.46 (Cairo Mus. cat.nos.52260,
52240, 52244) – amethyst and lapis lazuli
scarab rings (from the tomb of Queen Mereret
at Dahshur) on plain gold bases inscribed with
names and titles of Ammenemes III
(ca.1842–1797 BC).

Petrie, *Amulets*, 89h – a 'peridot' scarab with very similar markings (though the New Kingdom dating is doubtful).

*Kāmid el-Lōz* (1996) no.89ff. – unfinished scarabs dated to 2nd or 1st millennium BC, possibly locally made (p.129).

   nos.91, 95–6 – amethyst and two cornelians; bases uninscribed, plain plinths and simple linear markings on the backs.

   Egyptian, 12th Dynasty (or locally made?): about 1820 BC or later

**88**   5/1946.366 (Montague no.229, p.21) From Tripoli, Syria (see p.133)

**Pendant**, **bronze vase** or **amphora** with knob base and suspension ring on the top. 11 × 7mm

Publ.: *Bazaar*, 2/7/13, p.8, fig.12.

**88**                                             3:1

Amphora and amphora-like pendants were very common on Greek and Etruscan necklaces and earrings from the 6th to the 3rd centuries BC and their popularity continued into Roman times. They are found in a variety of forms (often with knob bases) and gold and silver examples are often very elaborate. Many amphora pendants come from Syria where the type continued into the 3rd and 4th centuries AD; on a relief from Palmyra (ca.AD 50–100) a seated goddess wears an earring with a plain amphora pendant (see M. Colledge, *The Art of Palmyra*, pl.38).

This simple amphora or vase-shaped pendant from Tripoli with its knob base, short neck and suspension ring above is closely related in type and shape to pendants found on many Phoenician and Punic sites round the Mediterranean. These pendants are more common in bone, ivory or glass but are also found in gold, silver and bronze. The slender shape of this amulet perhaps relates it more closely to Hellenistic *amphoriskoi* rather than the more rounded earlier types (cf. P. Fossing, *Glass Vessels before Glass-Blowing* (1940) pp.118–19, fig.92; also p.70, fig.45 (=Louvre, no.355) – for an example without handles (but of the more rounded shape dated 6th–4th century BC)). The vase seems to have been an important element in Punic imagery. It has been suggested that it might have had a libatory significance and was perhaps the symbol of a deity, possibly Tanit (*London Tharros* pp.88, 113).

Similar examples, sometimes without handles and often with a knob base, come from Phoenicio-Punic sites in Sardinia and elsewhere:

Acquaro, *Amuleti*, no.25 – bronze, 23 × 8mm; very similar but no excavation provenance.

*London Tharros*, pl.47a.4/24 – necklace with a silver vase-shaped pendant on the right, close in shape to the Exeter amulet (and a bronze example on the left) dated 5th/4th–3rdc. BC (Period IIb); note also the central pendant with a knob-based vase in granulated decoration (also pl.46.6/29).

   pl.126.27/18–19 – ivory vase pendants with knob bases and grooved necks.

L. Ruseva-Slokoska, *Roman Jewellery; a collection of the National Archaeological Museum – Sofia* (1991) p.209, no.291 – bronze, 17 × 2–5mm (similar to examples above) with knob base and flat round suspension hoop; found in a grave at Mezdra with other objects including a 4thc. AD coin – but the amulet could be earlier.

   Phoenician or Punic: 5th–3rd century BC

**89**  5/1946.364 (Montague no.227, p.21)
From Tripoli, Syria (see p.133)

**Two bronze fist amulets** (a & b) with holes for suspension.
(a) 16 × ca.7mm (b) 14 × ca.6mm (thickness ca.4mm)

Publ.: *Bazaar*, 2/7/13, p.8, fig.12

**89 (a)**                                         3:1

**89 (b)**

These two bronze clenched fist amulets with bracelets round the wrists could have been earring pendants or have formed part of a necklace. Although it is not clear whether the thumbs are between the first and second fingers they are probably related to the 'mano fica' type (**90**). Hand amulets of various types made in bone or ivory are usual in Phoenician contexts but examples in bronze seem unusual (see Acquaro, *Amuleti*, no.66ff.; *London Tharros*, pl.68b.15/22, i.23/23).

For similar clenched fists with bracelets round the wrist, see:

Acquaro, *Amuleti*, no.67 – bone.
*Vienna 3*, no.2446 – (1stc. BC?)–1stc. AD grey green serpentine.

    Phoenician: 5th–4th century BC (or Roman?)

**90**  5/1946.365 (Montague no.228, p.21)
From Tripoli, Syria (see p.133)

**'Mano fica' hand amulet**, faience, pale pinkish-white; hole for suspension.
18 × 8mm

Publ.: *Bazaar*, 2/7/13, p.8, fig.11

This '*mano fica*' – a clenched fist with the thumb between the first and second fingers – has three lines across the wrist and diagonal lines converging towards the palm. It is moulded in faience and has a perforation through the wrist from the side. The faience is very degraded but some patches of discoloured glaze remain on the back of the hand and in the recesses. (For faience see **91**.)

**90**                                         3:1

The hand making the 'fica' gesture has a very long history and is still used as an amulet today. Examples are found in many different materials and over a large area (see L. Hansmann & L. Kriss-Rettenbeck, *Amulett und Talisman* (1977) pp.199–201).

The meaning of the 'mano fica' is sometimes ambiguous but in antiquity it was most probably used as a symbolic representation of the female genitals and, like the phallus (**91**), was usually believed to have apotropaic qualities. An amulet combining both a phallus and 'mano fica' symbol makes this interpretation clear, see C. Johns, *Sex or Symbol* (1982), pp.72–3, fig.56. (For the meaning of the gesture see Elworthy, *Evil Eye*, pp.255–7; and C. Sourdive, *La Main dans l'Egypte Pharaonique* (1984) for the various types of hand amulet, including the 'mano fica', p.449.)

A number of faience 'mano fica' hand amulets come from Egypt and have usually been considered to be of Hellenistic or Roman date. However, earlier examples often made in bone or ivory are Phoenician and Punic (e.g. Acquaro, *Amuleti*, no.7off.; *London Tharros*, p.111).

For similar 'mano fica' amulets, mostly in faience and often found with associated types such as the phallus and altar (**91–2**) see:

*Berry Jewelry*, no.34 – 'Phoenician (?) or early Roman period (?)' frit and glass necklace with beads and pendants which include a 'Bes'-like figure, 'fica' hands, phallus amulets (**91**) and an altar or 'tooth' (**92**).

Elworthy, *Evil Eye*, p.135, fig.21 – necklace from Kertch with 'mano fica', phallus (**91**), altar (**92**) and other associated types.

S. Mollard-Besques, *Catalogue Raisonné des Figurines et Reliefs en Terre-cuite Grecs, Etrusques et Romains* iii (1972) pl.71a (Louvre nos.CA 245, 248) – faience amulets found in Kertch: a 'fica' hand and phallus (**91**) with associated types; 'Late Hellenistic, imported from Alexandria', 2nd–1stc. BC.

Sono, T. & Fukai, S. *Dailaman iii. Excavations at Hassani Mahale and Ghalekuti* (1964) p.61, pl.64, no.11 – faience fist; no.12 – phallus (**91**) on a bracelet from a tomb in N.W. Iran, dated 1st–3rdc. AD.

Rostovtzeff, *Dura Europos*, pp.126–7, pls.46,50 – faience 'fica' hand amulet, altar (**92**) and other associated types; dated 1st–3rdc. AD (i.e. pre-AD 256 when Dura Europos was sacked by Shapur I).

Cintas, *Amulettes* (1946) p.144 – a complete necklace from a tomb at Bembla in the Sahel with faience 'fica' hands, phalluses (**91**) and the usual related types dated to the end of the 1stc. BC.

*Naples* 1, nos.240,242 – similar 'fica' hand amulets from Pompeii (also nos.241,243–4); the phallus type (**91**) as well as Egyptian amulets such as 'Bes' are found at Herculaneum and Pompeii and so date to before the eruption in AD 79.

Dubin, *Beads*, Chart no.330 – pale blue faience from Iran, 'Parthian/Roman' period; (associated types nos.331–2, 341a,b,364–5).

Petrie, *Amulets*, nos.13a,b – dark blue glaze; from Egypt 'limited to the Roman period'.

Hansmann & Kriss-Rettenbeck, *op.cit.*, no.644 – Roman-Egyptian terracotta; very similar to the Exeter example.

Acquaro, *Amuleti*, no.72 – glass paste.

C. Johns, *Sex or Symbol* (1982) pl.10 – a Roman gold 'mano fica' amulet.

Phoenician, Hellenistic or Roman: 6th–5th century BC onwards

**91**  5/1946.370 (Montague no.233, p.21)
Found in Tripoli, Syria (see p.133)

**Two faience phallic amulets** (a & b) with holes for suspension.
(a) 18 × 11 × 7mm flat back; pale green
(b) 17 × 13 × 5mm as above but a more degraded, rougher surface

**91 (a)** (see also frontispiece)                    3:1

**91 (b)**                    3:1

Like the 'mano fica' (**90**), this type of amulet, though found in Egypt, is not considered to be typically Egyptian. Although phallic objects were made in Egypt from the New Kingdom (i.e. from ca.1550 BC), phallic material of this sort (including **90,92**) associated with Bes who was linked with human fertility is usually believed to date from the Greco-Roman period (see G. Pinch, *Votive Offerings to Hathor* (1993), p.235ff., pp.239–40, 245). Examples (usually in bone or ivory), however, have been found on Phoenician and Punic sites round the Mediterranean and these amulets have been dated earlier (see *London Tharros*, pp.42,111).

Faience is of Egyptian origin and moulded amulets belonging to the Egyptian repertoire were thought to have been made in the Delta and exported to Carthage in the 7th and 6th centuries BC. Later these typically Egyptian amulets were probably copied at Punic and Phoenician centres round the Mediterranean and elsewhere, and then made alongside amulets considered to be non-Egyptian such as these two phallic amulets, the 'mano fica' (**90**) and the 'altar' (**92**).

These three types are often found in association with each other, as well as with more typically Egyptian amulets such as scarabs, fluted vases, bunches of grapes, 'Bes' or 'Bes'-like figures (see refs. for **90,92**). Faience amulets are very common and were widely traded throughout the Mediterranean and the Middle East but, of course, their colour and composition varies and there are slight differences in design. Examples have been found on sites as far apart as Pompeii, Iran, Kertch,

and Central Asia (see D. Harden, *The Phoenicians* (1962) pp.90,155,162,193; and examples given for **90,92**). Cintas suggests that as faith in the gods declined in the late Punic period, the 'fica' hand, phallus and altar, which had a mainly prophylactic purpose, became more common (see Cintas, *Amulettes*, pl.26, p.141ff.).

For similar phallic amulets, mostly in faience (often found with associated types, including **90,92**) see:

*Berry Jewelry*, see ref. **90**.
Elworthy, *Evil Eye*, see ref. **90**.
Mollard-Besques, see *op.cit.* **90**.
Sono & Fukai, see *op.cit.* **90**.
Rostovtzeff, *Dura Europos*, pls.43–4,54 – with other faience amulets; pp.126–7; cf. **90**.
Cintas, *Amulettes*, see ref. **90**.
*Naples* 1, nos.229,236,364 – very like (a);
    no.230 a similar type to (b); (nos.231–5,363,365 similar).
    (See under *Naples* 1, **90** for associated types.)
Dubin, *Beads*, Chart no.341a (associated types nos.330–2,341b).
*Ornament* 6, no.4 (1983), p.45 – glass and moulded faience examples from N.W. Iran.
Petrie, *Amulets*, nos.16a,b – examples in blue glass and red glass, 'Roman'.
*London Tharros*, pl.681.26/25 – green glazed composition of Egyptian appearance; this is dated by Acquaro to the 6th c. BC (p.42).
Acquaro, *Amuleti*, no.79 – a Phoenician example in ivory.
C. Johns, *Sex or Symbol*, pl.10 – similar phallic symbols in gold.

Phoenician, Hellenistic or Roman: 6th–5th century BC onwards

**92** 5/1946.367 (a) & 5/1946.368 (b)
(Montague nos.230–1, p.21)
From Tripoli, Syria (see p.133)

### Two bronze horned altar amulets

(a & b) with holes for suspension.
(a) Patches of red patination.
11 × 6mm
(b) Corroded surface with some red patches.
9 × 5–6mm

Publ.: *Bazaar*, 2/7/13, p.8, fig.11

These 'horned altar' amulets (sometimes described as 'fire altars' or 'tooth' amulets) are made in various materials. Many altar amulets were made in faience and are found in association with the more common 'mano fica' and phallic amulets described here (**90,91**).

**92 (a)**

**92 (b)**                                        3:1

This type of amulet is usually thought to represent a horned altar though when suspended on a necklace it would hang upside down. (Punic altar amulets are slightly different, see *London Tharros*, p.112).
   The square four-horned altar is mentioned in the Bible (1 Kings 1:50, 2:28) and an actual example in stone (very close in shape to this

amulet) dates back to before the 8th century BC (see B. Trell, 'The Coins of the Phoenician World – East and West' in *Ancient Coins of the Graeco-Roman World – The Nickle Numismatic Papers* ed. W. Heckel & R. Sullivan (1984) p.121, no.23 and for other examples no.24ff.). It is believed that horned altars are of Syrian origin and they are common in the Syrio-Phoenician region. (An example from Gezer is dated to 600 BC – see W. Deonna, 'Mobilier Délien' II, *BCH* 58 (1934) pp.405–6; numerous examples of horned altars of all types and sizes and in various materials are cited in this article, pp.381–447.)
   During the Hellenistic period (from the 3rd century BC) horned altars appeared in Egypt where they continued into the Christian era (4th–5th century AD). They became very widespread and examples in stone (as well as smaller portable altars) were found in Egyptian sanctuaries associated with the Isiac cult in Delos, Pompeii, Alexandria and elsewhere. They were used for burning incense in the performance of Greco-Egyptian cults and also funerary rites.
   A very well-preserved example still stands outside the tomb of Petosiris; it is dated about 300 BC (see G. Lefebvre, *Le Tombeau de Petosiris* (1923) I, p.13, fig.2). A flaming horned altar stands between Ptolemy II and Arsinoe on a relief dated 270–246 BC (see J. Quaegebeur, 'Ptolemée II en adoration devant Arsinoé II divinisée', *BIFAO* 69 (1971) pp.195–7, pl.29 (Pushkin Mus. no.5375). (For horned altars in Egypt see G. Soukiassian, 'Les autels "à cornes" ou "à acrotères" en Égypte', *BIFAO* 83 (1983) pp.317–33.)

For horned altar amulets in bronze and other materials, often with associated types (including the 'mano fica' and phallus, **90–1**) see:

*Berry Jewelry*, see ref. **90**.
Elworthy, *Evil Eye*, see ref. **90**.
Rostovtzeff, *Dura Europos*, see pl.46 – faience altar, 'fica' hand (see **90**) and associated types.
Dubin, *Beads*, Chart nos.364–5 – stone examples from Iran dated ca.300 AD.
*Ornament* 8, no.4 (1985) p.67, fig.1 – three altar ('ancient tooth') amulets in faience, bronze and rock crystal from the Middle East.
*London Tharros*, pl.68n – an ivory altar, rather different in shape and with a suspension ring on the top, but probably horned.

Phoenician, Hellenistic or Roman: 6th–5th
century BC onwards

**93**   5/1946.369 (Montague no.232, p.21)
From Tripoli, Syria (see p.133)

**Glass pendant** perforated for suspension at the top.
34 × 5mm (at end)

Publ.: *Bazaar*, 2/7/13, p.8, fig.11

The pendant is pale blue with an iridescent surface; striations and grooves run along its length.

**93**                    3:1

centre and widen towards the lower end (see below). Bronze bells have been found on many Punic sites (*London Tharros*, p.45) and probably date from the 5th–3rd century BC, but perhaps continued into the 1st century BC. Bells had an amuletic or ritual function and it was believed that the sound frightened off evil spirits. A glass bell pendant made without a clapper was excavated at Ste. Monique which suggests that bells need not always have a functional purpose but could be purely symbolic (Cintas, *Amulettes*, pp.89–90). It is possible that clappers worn on their own might have also had this symbolic function.

Compare:

P. Bartoloni, *Rivista di Studi Fenici* 1 (1973) 'Gli amuleti Punici del *tofet* di Sulcis', pl.63,4 (p.201, no.90) – bronze bell clapper (32.5 × 7mm)

   Phoenicio-Punic?: 5th–1st century BC?

Many glass obelisk-shaped pendants with square or rectangular shafts (possibly of phallic significance) have been found on Punic sites (see *London Tharros*, pp.112–13). The shape of this glass pendant is unusual. Montague thought it was phallic but in both size and shape it resembles bronze bell clappers which become narrow in the

**94**   5/1946.371 (Montague no.234, p.21)

**Phallus pendant**, (talc?), slightly greenish with beige patches; a suspension hole at the top.
35 × 10mm

Compare:

*London Tharros*, pl.113.20/23 – necklace with a pendant phallus of similar type in reddish composition but the suspension hole passes through the body of the amulet two thirds of the way up; the central pendant of the necklace is dated to the 5thc. BC.
Petrie, *Amulets*, no.16e – similar amulet but green glazed; 'Greco-Roman'.

Phoenician or Punic: about 5th century BC or later (?)

**95**   5/1946.381 (Montague no.237, p.22)
Found in Palestine

**Bead, etched cornelian**; irregular shape, perforated horizontally; chipped round the edge, on the face and round the perforation.
ca.14mm (diam.) × 7mm

This etched cornelian bead has a simple white 6-pointed star design on both sides with a dot in the space between each line.

**94**                                        3:1

**95**                                        4:1

Montague suggested that this phallus pendant was Egyptian and attributes it to the 17th Dynasty (ca.1650–1550 BC). Although votive phalluses have been found in Egypt, amulets of this sort seem unusual (see remarks for **91**). A few, however, do come from Punic sites (see *London Tharros*, p.111). Many Punic amulets have the suspension hole passing through a narrow area cut away at the top as it is here (cf. Acquaro, *Amuleti*, p.16 & n.15, nos.70,73).

The earliest etched cornelian beads date back to before 2000 BC and were probably made at Ur and Kish from where they were exported to

India and perhaps elsewhere. This example corresponds in design to Beck's Middle Period (ca.300 BC–AD 200) where the beads have a regular geometric pattern of straight lines. It belongs to the most common type where the pattern is painted with alkali (soda) on the cornelian and then fired to turn it white (see H. Beck, 'Etched cornelian beads' *Ant. Jnl.* 13 (1933) pp.384–98, where he identifies two methods of etching and divides the beads into three broad chronological groups according to design (pl.71); also J. Reade, *Early Etched Beads and the Indus-Mesopotamia Trade*, Occasional Paper no.2 British Museum, 1979). (The less usual types of etched beads are black on white, or black on red.)

Compare:

Beck, *op.cit.*, pl.67, fig.5 (first example) – a bead of about the same size and with the same pattern but black on white (Type 2); 'from India'.

Dubin, *Beads*, p.16 – a group of etched cornelian beads of various shapes and designs from Parthian and Sassanian sites in Iran dated from 249 BC to AD 642 but a few appear to belong to the Early Period. The example on the top left and bottom right are close to the Exeter type. (Content collection.)

About 300 BC–AD 200 (Beck's Middle Period)

**96**                                                    3:1

**96**  5/1946.373 (Montague no.236, p.21)

**Lead amulet**, circular, double-sided; a stinging insect (a wasp or bee?) on one side and a scorpion on the other; both surrounded by a beaded border. (Four symmetrically placed holes on the scorpion side.)
22mm (diam.) × ca.4mm

Publ.: *Bazaar*, 13/1/12, p.88, fig.3.

This is probably an amulet to protect against stinging insects. The amulet seems unusual but single- and double-sided lead tokens were found on the Athenian Agora (M. Lang & M. Crosby,

*The Athenian Agora* 10 (1964) 'Weights, Measures and Tokens' – Hellenistic tokens, p.92ff. and Roman, p.109ff. These tokens are rather smaller but some examples have insects on them (e.g. L73 B – a bee (?)).

Scorpions, bees and wasps are common on engraved gems from the earliest times. Scorpions were the most feared invertebrates in antiquity but bees were popular insects and were considered less aggressive than wasps (see *Greek Insects*, pp.21, 47–83). If the purpose of this amulet was to protect against stinging insects, a wasp combined with a scorpion might be more appropriate than a bee.

A common type of Roman apotropaic amulet has a human eye in the centre surrounded by pointed objects, wild animals and stinging insects. These are often disc-shaped with beading round the edge. Compare amulets and gems:

P.W. Schienerl, 'The Much-Enduring Eye', *Ornament* 7, no.4 (1984) p.27, Figs.1,3 – gold medallions from Sicily and Herculaneum.
   Fig.4 – the same motif on a gem which includes a bee and scorpion surrounding the eye.
*Würzburg*, no.648 (Florence: Migliarini, no.3237) – 1st century AD gem, as Fig.4 above.

Hellenistic, Roman or Byzantine

**97**    5/1946.361 (Montague no.224, p.21)
From Athens?

**Cameo, eye/face amulet,** layered or 'eyed' agate (grey/white translucent chalcedony) cut in a drop shape.
19 × 16 × 6mm flat back, convex face
Mount: modern silver ring, ht.20mm (inc. stone) × w.17mm; hoop: plano-convex w.5mm.

The stone is cut so that the eyes are in the lighter-coloured layers of the stone; and with the wedge-shaped beak or nose it gives the impression of an owl head or a human face seen from the front.

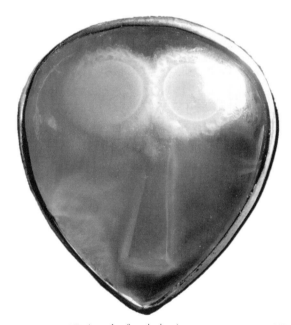

**97** (see also frontispiece)       4:1

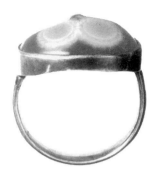

2:1

Frontal owls' heads were common on cameos and intaglios in all periods (*Hermitage Intaglios*, no.8 – 6thc. BC; E. Babelon, *Catalogue des camées antiques et modernes de la Bibliothèque Nationale* (1897) no.202; *Romania*, no.952 – two-layered yellow and white onyx).

This amulet is difficult to date but seems more closely related to the eye beads (usually single but sometimes double) cut from layered agate which had been used for apotropaic effect in Western Asia from about the 3rd millennium BC. They became very widespread and by the mid 1st millennium BC appear in Europe.

There is no close parallel for this stone, but compare:

Dubin, *Beads*, p.311, fig.329.6 – layered cornelian/chalcedony double eye bead, though without a 'nose' or 'beak'; from Western Asia dated 3rd–1st millennium BC.

*The Malcove Collection* (1985) ed. S.D. Campbell, no.1 – an animal/bird mask cut in dark stone and triangular in shape from Anatolia, dated 'probably 4th–3rd millennium BC' has a similar appearance and 'probably served as an amulet . . . possibly a deity of some kind'.

Date uncertain: perhaps 1st millennium BC or later (modern?)

**98**  5/1946.352 (Montague no.215, p.19)

**Bronze cross** with perforations at the end of the two long arms.
31 × 21 × ca.5–7mm

The cross is oval in section with a flattened area round the perforations. This suggests that it may have been a link in a chain for suspending a lamp or censer rather than for wearing as a pendant (see S.D. Campbell, *op.cit.* below).

**98**                                                          3:1

This cross corresponds to types dated to the 5th century or later from the East Mediterranean:

*Byzantium at Princeton; Byzantine Art and Archaeology at Princeton Museum* (1986) eds. S. Ćurčić & A. St Clair, nos.76–7 – small bronze pendant crosses, elliptical in section.

*The Malcove Collection* (1985) ed. S.D. Campbell, nos.116–17 – Byzantine/Coptic lamps or censers dated 5th/6th and 6th/7thc. AD with crosses as links in the suspension chains.

nos.142–8 – Byzantine bronze pendant crosses; no.144 with the ends of the arms rounded; dated possibly 7th–8thc. AD (the same types were excavated at Aphrodisias in Caria associated with tombs dated to 6th–8th century).

*Byzantium* (1994) ed. D. Buckton, no.113a – copper alloy censer ca. mid 6th–7thc. AD with crosses in the suspension chain. From Syria.

Byzantine 6th–8th century AD

**99**   5/1946.382 (Montague, no.238, p.22)

**Glass stamp**, pale milky green, translucent; the surface worn and pitted with some iron-staining.
diam.19–20 × 4mm; weight 2.67g

*Islamic glass stamp* or *coin weight* with raised border and three horizontal lines of illegible inscription on the obverse; the reverse unstamped. Probably from Egypt.

**99**                                                    3:1

The first datable glass stamps known from Egypt after the Islamic conquest are of the early 8th century AD and their production continued until the 14th or 15th century. These derive from the earlier Byzantine glass stamps or disks which have been found in Egypt. The legends on many stamps describe what they were for and who issued them. They were used for various (and sometimes unknown) purposes but the majority were produced by the office of weights and measures. The smaller ones were mostly coin weights, used for checking the weight of the gold, silver and copper coins and their fractions – *dinars, dirhams* and *fulūs* (see A.H. Morton, *A Catalogue of Early Islamic Glass Stamps in the British Museum* (1985) p.9ff.). Legends are not always explicit and it is uncertain whether the smaller disks were always used as coin weights. Some small disks were probably tokens of some sort as, although they are from the same die, they vary greatly in weight. It has even been suggested that they were amulets for political propaganda.

There has been some controversy over whether later Fātimid stamps were used as coin weights or actually replaced currency when copper was in short supply. There are plausible arguments to support both theories (see P. Balog, 'The Fātimid Glass Jeton', *Annali, Istituto Italiano di Numismatica* 18–19 (1971–2) pp.175–64 and 20 (1973) pp.121–212; M. Bates, 'The Function of Fātimid and Ayyūbid Glass Weights', and P. Balog, 'Fātimid Glass Jetons: Token Currency or Coin-Weights?', *Journal of Economic and Social History of the Orient* 24 (1981) pp.63–92 and 93–109. See also Morton, *op.cit.* p.14ff. for earlier coin weights).

The legend stamped on this example is unfortunately illegible. Its weight (2.67g) is rather less than the single *dirham* standard of 2.97g though close in weight (but not size) to the *dirham* weights of 13–*kharruba* (cf. Morton, *op.cit.*, pp.16–18).

It appears to resemble some Fātimid weights:

S. Lane-Poole, *Catalogue of Glass Weights in the British Museum* (1891) no.335 (cf. pl.7.332) – a *dirham* weight (2.98g) of the Fātimid caliph al-ᶜAdid (1160–71); similar opaque glass weight with three lines of inscription.

G. Förschner, *Glaspasten, geschnittene Steine, arabische Münzegewichte* (1982) no.15 – Fātimid period, mid 10th–mid 12thc. AD greenish white opaque *dirham* weight (3.03g) with imitation legend in horizontal lines (see also P. Balog, *op.cit.* 20 (1973), pl.23).

Fātimid, 10th–12th century AD

**100**  86/1966 (Corkill, M.13)
From Tello(?)

**Disc-shaped bead** with inscription, mottled cloudy agate (or cornelian), pale pinkish/orange with red specks on the underside; highly polished but uneven face.
diam.13 × ht.5/8mm

*Bead* with Arabic inscription (in positive) reading: ya 'ali – 'Oh! Ali!' – Invocation of the Prophet Muhammad's son-in-law who was the first Shi'te Imam.

**101**  86/1966 (Corkill, M.3)
From Tello(?)

**Spindle whorl**, microgranite or microsyenite (tested); low cone with perforation from apex to base.
diam.ca.30 × ht.9mm
diam. of perforation 7mm

*Spindle whorl* with seven characters inscribed round the edge of the upper side; three small holes round the perforation on the underside (or flaws in the stone?).

**100**                        3:1

The bead itself may be much earlier than the inscription. Although the upper surface is highly polished it is not level. The bead probably comes from Southern Iraq or Iran.

18th–19th century

**101**                        3:1

Lionel Giles in a letter written from the British Museum (24/4/30) to C.J. Gadd attempts a reading but says he is 'doubtful about this inscription being meant for Chinese, though some of the characters are legible as such . . . The only character which is certainly Chinese as it stands is 月 "moon".'

The inscription has still not been identified and as the shapes of the signs are rather general they could represent variants of several writing systems. Some of the characters, though, do appear similar to late archaic Chinese writing dating to sometime after the 3rd century BC. The inscription as a whole, however, cannot be read at the moment. Likewise a number of the characters could be considered variants of Indus signs individually, but their sequences and orientations are atypical of the Indus script (late 3rd or early 2nd millennium BC).

(It is intended to publish this spindle whorl in A. Parpola, B.M. Pande & P. Koskikallio (eds.), *Corpus of Indus Seals and Inscriptions* vol.3: New Material . . . (Helsinki: 1998(?) forthcoming.)

Uncertain

**102**   5/1946.602 (Montague no.469, p.44)

**Chalcedony** with horizontal white layers running parallel to the surface on one side; roughly shaped oval, flat face and back. ca.25 × 20 × 10mm

**102**                                               3:1

Montague in his catalogue suggests this is a 'Roman gem-stone, 1in × .8in, in process of cutting, probably for an intaglio'. This stone has been neatly chipped into shape with smooth concoidal fractures. After polishing (cf. **103**) it could have been used for an intaglio or perhaps a bead. (Beads were perforated before the final polishing.)

In India semi-precious stones are still prepared for bead-making or engraving as they were in antiquity. Duller grey or yellowish white specimens of chalcedony (like this stone) are sometimes heated to change the colour to the more sought-after red or orange cornelian. Heating also drives off the intergranular water molecules and softens the silica which makes chipping easier.

These processes and the tools used are described in R.V. Karanth, 'The Ancient Gem Industry in Cambay', *Man and Environment* 27 (1) (1992) pp.61–9; and V. Roux 'Le travail des lapidaires; atelier de Khambhat (Cambay): passé et présent', *Les pierres précieuses de l'Orient ancien des Sumériens aux Sassanides* (49 Exposition-dossier du département des Antiquités orientales du musée du Louvre: Paris 1995) pp.39–44.

Roman or modern?

**103**  5/1946.718 (Montague no.573, p.56)
From William Green (see pp.131–2)

**Cornelian** or '**sard**' (A.4) with white patches (etching) on the upper face and on the edge.
9 × 7 × 4mm

**103**                                                          4:1

The stone is shaped and polished, perhaps in preparation for engraving. White patches or etching can be produced artificially or, as is more likely to be the case here, can occur naturally during burial (see M. Sax, 'Recognition and Nomenclature of Quartz Materials with specific reference to Engraved Gemstones', *Jewellery Studies* 7 (1996) pp.66–7; and cf. the intentionally etched bead, **95**). For the working of stone see references for **102**.

Date unknown

# ABBREVIATIONS AND SELECT BIBLIOGRAPHY

Acquaro, *Amuleti* –
E. Acquaro, *Amuleti Egiziani ed Egittizzanti del Museo Nazionale di Cagliari* (1977)

*(AGDS) Berlin* etc. –
*Antike Gemmen in deutschen Sammlungen* – see *Berlin, Brunswick, Göttingen, Hamburg, Hanover, Kassel, Munich*

*AG* –
A. Furtwängler, *Die Antiken Gemmen 1–3* (1900)

*AGGems* –
J. Boardman, *Archaic Greek Gems, Schools and Artists in the Sixth and Early Fifth Centuries BC* (1968)

Aldred, *Jewels* –
C. Aldred, *Jewels of the Pharaohs* (1971)

Andrews, *Amulets* –
C. Andrews, *Amulets of Ancient Egypt* (1994)

Andrews, *Jewellery* –
C. Andrews, *Ancient Egyptian Jewellery* (1990)

*Ant. Jnl.* –
*The Antiquaries Journal, being the Journal of the Society of Antiquaries of London*

*Aquileia* –
G. Sena Chiesa, *Gemme del Museo Nazionale di Aquileia* (1966)

*Bari* –
G. Tamma, *Le Gemme del Museo Archeologico di Bari* (1991)

*Bazaar* –
*Bazaar, the Exchange and Mart* (1868– )

*BCH* –
*Bulletin de correspondence hellénique*

*Berlin* –
E. Zwierlein-Diehl, *Antike Gemmen in deutschen Sammlungen 2: Berlin* (1969)

*BerlinVARS* –
A. Moortgat, *Vorderasiatische Rollsiegel*, Berlin (1940)

*Berry Jewelry* –
W. & E. Rudolf, *Ancient Jewelry from the Collection of Burton Y. Berry* (1973)

*BIFAO* –
*Bulletin de l'Institut français d'archéologie orientale*

*BMC . . . –*
British Museum Catalogue (of Coins)

*BMC Empire –*
H. Mattingly & R.A.G. Carson, *Coins of the Roman Empire in the British Museum* 1–6 (1923–1964)

*BN/LouvreSass –*
R. Gyselen, *Catalogue des sceaux, camées, et bulles sassanides de la Bibliothèque Nationale et du Musée du Louvre*, 1. Collection Général (1994), 2. P. Gignoux, Les sceaux et bulles inscrits (1978)

Bonner, *SMA –*
C. Bonner, *Studies in Magical Amulets, chiefly Graeco-Egyptian. University of Michigan Studies Humanistic Series* 49 (1950)

Borisov & Lukonin –
A.Y. Borisov & B.G. Lukonin, *Sasanidskiye Gemmi* (1963)

*Britain –*
M. Henig, *A Corpus of Roman Engraved Gemstones from British Sites*, in *BAR* 8 (2nd ed. 1978)

*Caerleon –*
J.D. Zienkiewicz, *The Legionary Fortress Baths at Caerleon. 2 The Finds* (1986)

*Cambridge –*
M. Henig & M. Whiting, *Classical Gems: Ancient and Modern Intaglios and Cameos in the Fitzwilliam Museum, Cambridge* (1994)

*Cintas, Amulettes –*
P. Cintas, *Amulettes Puniques* (1946)

*Cologne –*
A. Krug, 'Antike Gemmen in Römisch-Germanischen Museum Köln' in *Bericht der Römische-Germanischen Kommission* 61 (1980)

*Content Cameos –*
M. Henig, *The Content Family Collection of Ancient Cameos* (1990)

*Corpus –*
E. Porada, *Corpus of Near Eastern Seals in North American Collections* 1, *The Pierpoint Morgan Library Collection* (1948)

*Dalmatian Gems –*
S. Hoey Middleton, *Engraved Gems from Dalmatia, from the Collections of Sir John Gardner Wilkinson and Sir Arthur Evans in Harrow School, at Oxford and elsewhere* (1991)

Delatte/Derchain –
A. Delatte & P. Derchain, *Bibliothèque Nationale. Les intailles magiques gréco-égyptiennes* (1964)

Delaporte 1–2 –
L. Delaporte, *Musée du Louvre, Catalogue des cylindres, cachets et pierres gravées de style oriental*: 1, *Fouilles et missions* (1920); 2, *Acquisitions* (1923)

Dubin, *Beads –*
L. Sherr Dubin, *The History of Beads: from 30,000 BC to the Present* (1987)

*EGAZ* –
R.M. Boehmer, *Die Entwicklung der Glyptik während der Akkad-Zeit* (1965)

Elworthy, *Evil Eye* –
T. Elworthy, *The Evil Eye* (1895)

*Expert* –
*The Expert*, 1907–9

F.*Berlin* –
A. Furtwängler, *Königliche Museen zu Berlin. Beschreibung der geschnittenen Steine im Antiquarium* (1896)

*FI* –
D. Collon, *First Impressions: Cylinder Seals in the Ancient Near East* (1987)

Frankfort –
H. Frankfort, *Cylinder Seals* (1939)

*Gaul* –
H. Guiraud, *Intailles et camées de l'époque romaine en Gaule* (1988)

*Geneva* –
M.-L. Vollenweider, *Musée d'art et d'histoire de Genève. Catalogue raisonné des sceaux, cylindres, intailles et camées*
1–3 (1967, 1979, 1983)

*Getty* –
J. Speir, *Ancient Gems and Finger Rings* (1992)

*GGFR* –
J. Boardman, *Greek Gems and Finger Rings, Early Bronze Age to Late Classical* (1970)

*GM* –
A. Parrot, *Glyptique mésopotamienne* (1954)

*GMA* –
P. Amiet, *La glyptique mésopotamienne archaïque* 2nd ed. (1980)

Göbl –
R. Göbl, *Der Sāsānidische Siegelkanon* (1973)

*Göttingen* –
P. Gercke, *Antike Gemmen in deutschen Sammlungen 3: Goettingen* (1970)

*Greek Insects* –
M. Davies & J. Kathirithamby, *Greek Insects* (1986)

*Hague* –
M. Maaskant-Kleibrink, *Catalogue of the Engraved Gems in the Royal Coin Cabinet, The Hague* (1978)

*Hamburg* –
M. Schlüter, G. Platz-Horster, P. Zazoff, *Antike Gemmen in deutschen Sammlungen 4: Hamburg* (1975)

*Hanover* –
M. Schlüter, G. Platz-Horster, P. Zazoff, *Antike Gemmen in deutschen Sammlungen 4: Hannover* (1975)

*Heeramaneck –*
P.R.S. Moorey et al, *Ancient Bronzes, Ceramics and Seals. The Heeramaneck Collection* (1981)

Henkel –
F. Henkel, *Die römischen Fingerringe der Rheinlande und der benachbarten Gebiete* (1913)

*Hermitage Intaglios –*
O. Neverov, *Antique Intaglios in the Hermitage Collection* (1976)

Hornbostel, *Sarapis –*
W. Hornbostel, *Sarapis* (1973)

*Intaglios and Rings –*
J. Boardman, *Intaglios and Rings, Greek, Etruscan and Eastern from a private collection* (1975)

*Ionides –*
J. Boardman, *Engraved Gems, the Ionides Collection* (1968)

*JHS –*
*Journal of Hellenic Studies*

*JRA –*
*Journal of Roman Archaeology*

*Kāmid el-Lōz* (1996) –
H. Kühne & B. Salje, 'Kāmid el-Lōz.' 15. Glyptik. *Saarbrüker Beiträge zur Altertumskunde* 56 (1996)

*Kassel –*
P. Zazoff, *Antike Gemmen in deutschen Sammlungen 3: Kassel* (1970)

Kent, *RC –*
J.P.C. Kent, *Roman Coins* (1978)

*Koch –*
A.B. Chadour, *Ringe . . . =Rings: The Alice and Louis Koch Collection* (1994)

*Lewis –*
M. Henig, *The Lewis Collection of Engraved Gemstones in Corpus Christi College, Cambridge*, in *BAR* Int. Ser., 1 (1975)

*LIMC –*
*Lexicon Iconographicum Mythologiae Classicae* (1981– )

*London –*
H.B. Walters, *Catalogue of the Engraved Gems and Cameos, Greek, Etruscan and Roman in the British Museum* (1926)

*LondonRings –*
F.H. Marshall, *Catalogue of the Finger Rings, Greek, Etruscan and Roman, British Museum* (1907)

*LondonSass –*
A.D.H. Bivar, *Catalogue of the Western Asiatic Seals in the British Museum. Stamp Seals II, the Sassanian Dynasty* (1969)

*London Tharros* –
R.D. Barnett & C. Mendleson, *Tharros: A Catalogue of Material in the British Museum from Phoenician and other Tombs at Tharros, Sardinia* (1987)

*London WA* –
D.J. Wiseman, *Catalogue of the Western Asiatic Seals in the British Museum . . .* 1 (1962), D. Collon, 2 (1982), 3 (1986)

*Luni* –
G. Sena Chiesa, *Gemme di Luni* (1978)

*Malter 58* (1994) –
Malter Galleries Inc. & L. Alexander Wolfe, *6,000 Years of Seals*, Auction 58, Encino, California (1994)

*Marcopoli* –
B. Tessier, *Ancient Near Eastern Cylinder Seals from the Marcopoli Collection* (1984)

*Merz* –
M.-L. Vollenweider, *Deliciae Leonis – Antike geschnittene Steine und Ringe aus eine Privatsammlung* (1984)

*Mira et Magica* –
H. Philipp, *Mira et Magica: Gemmen im Ägyptischen Museum der Staatlichen Museen Preussischer Kulturbesitz, Berlin-Charlottenburg* (1986)

*Munich* –
*Antike Gemmen in deutschen Sammlungen 1*: i – E. Brandt; ii – E. Brandt, E. Schmidt; iii – E. Brandt, A. Krug, W. Gercke, E. Schmidt: *Munich* (1968–1972)

*Naples* –
U. Pannuti, *Museo Archeologico Nazionale di Napoli: Catalogo della collezione glittica* 1 (1983), 2 (1994)

*Nijmegen* –
M. Maaskant-Kleibrink, *Description of the Collections in the Rijksmuseum G.M. Kam at Nijmegen, X. The Engraved Gems, Roman and non-Roman* (1986)

*N.Y.* –
G.M.A. Richter, *Catalogue of Engraved Gems: Greek, Etruscan and Roman. Metropolitan Museum of Art, New York* (1956)

*N.Y. Sas* –
C.J. Brunner, *Sasanian Stamp Seals in the Metropolitan Museum of Art, New York* (1980)

*Oxford* –
J. Boardman & M.-L. Vollenweider, *Catalogue of the Engraved Gems and Finger Rings*: 1 *Greek and Etruscan* (1978)

*Oxford ANE* –
B. Buchanan, *Catalogue of the Ancient Near Eastern Seals in the Ashmolean Museum* 1 (1966); B. Buchanan & P.R.S. Moorey, *The Iron Age Stamp Seals* 3 (1988)

Petrie, *Amulets* –
W.M.F. Petrie, *Amulets* (1914)

*QAN* –
R.N. Frye, *Sasanian Remains from Qasr-i Abu Nasr: Seals, Sealings and Coins* (1973)

*RIB* –
R.G. Collingwood & R.P. Wright, *The Roman Inscriptions of Britain* 2 'Instrumentum Domesticum' . . . Fascicule i (. . . Lead sealings) (eds) S.S. Frere, M. Roxan & R.S.O. Tomlin (1990); Fascicule iii (Brooches, rings, gems . . .) (eds) S.S. Frere and R.S.O. Tomlin (1991)

*RIC* –
H. Mattingly, E.A. Sydenham, C.H.V. Sutherland & R.A.G. Carson, *Roman Imperial Coinage* 1–9 (1923–1981)

Richter 1 –
G.M.A. Richter, *Engraved Gems of the Greeks and the Etruscans* (1968)

Richter 2 –
G.M.A. Richter, *Engraved Gems of the Romans* (1971)

*Romania* –
M. Gramatopol, 'Les Pierres gravées du Cabinet numismatique de l'Académie Roumaine', *Collection Latomus* 138 (1974)

Rostovtzeff, *Dura Europos* –
M. Rostovtzeff, *Excavations at Dura Europos* Preliminary Report of the 9th season, 1935–6, pt.ii, the Necropolis.

*Sa'd* –
M. Henig & M. Whiting, *Engraved Gems from Gadara in Jordan: the Sa'd Collection of Intaglios and Cameos* (1985)

*Sofia* –
A. Dimitrova-Milcheva, *Antique Engraved Gems and Cameos in the National Archaeological Museum in Sofia* (1981)

*Thorvaldsen* –
P. Fossing, *The Thorvaldsen Museum. Catalogue of the Antique Engraved Gems and Cameos* (1929)

*Vienna* –
E. Zwierlein-Diehl, *Die antiken Gemmen des Kunsthistorischen Museums in Wien* 1–3 (1973, 1979, 1991)

*Würzburg* –
E. Zwierlein-Diehl, *Glaspasten im Martin-Von-Wagner Museum der Universität Würzburg* 1 – *Abdrücke von antiken und ausgewählten nachantiken Intagli und Kameen* (1986)

*Yale* –
B. Buchanan, *Early Near Eastern Seals in the Yale Babylonian Collection* (1981)

## COLLECTIONS, COLLECTORS, DEALERS AND AUCTIONEERS

*Babington, Revd Dr Churchill* (1821–1889):
   see **30**, **72**, **80**, **83**:
Churchill Babington was born at Roecliffe in Leicestershire on 11 March 1821, the son of the Revd Matthew Drake Babington. He was admitted to St John's College Cambridge in 1839 and graduated in 1843, being awarded a 1st in the Classical Tripos. In 1846 he travelled to Messina and Naples where he studied botany and Roman antiquities. He was elected a Fellow of the College and ordained in 1846; from 1865–80 he was Disney Professor of Archaeology. Babington contributed articles to learned journals on many subjects, including numismatics, archaeology, philology, botany, and ornithology. A number of the entries in Smith and Cheetham's *Dictionary of Christian Antiquities* (1880) are by him – including those on gems, medals, glass, inscriptions, seals and rings. In 1866 he left Cambridge and accepted the rectory of Cockfield in Suffolk.

   He left his Greek vases to the Fitzwilliam Museum, Cambridge. 'A few antiquities, gems cylinders, etc. of the Late Revd Dr Churchill Babington' were sold by Sotheby's on 9 April 1891 with the collection of the Revd W.F. Short. (For **72**, **80**, **83** see also *Clements, Luther* below.)

   See entries and obituaries in: *Alumni Cantabrigiensis* (comp. J.A. Venn) 1 pt.ii, 1752–1900 (CUP 1940); *DNB* 22, (suppl.1909); *Guardian*, 15 January 1889; *Eagle*, 15 March 1889; *Proc. Suffolk Instit. of Archaeol. & Nat. Hist.*, 7 pt.i (1891) pp.xix–xxi.

*Clements, Luther:*
(or 'L. Clements', *Bazaar*, 2 July 1913; presumably also the 'Clements' referred to elsewhere):
   see **27**, **67–8**, **72**, **78**, **80**, **83**
Montague purchased engraved gems and other antiquities from Clements who appears to have been a dealer. The name 'Clements' is frequently written in the margins of annotated auction catalogues – including the Foster's catalogue for the *Odescalchi* sale (see below) at which he bought several lots.

*Evans, Sir Arthur John* (1851–1941):
   see **37–8**, **40**, **45**
Explorer, writer, archaeologist, and Keeper of the Ashmolean Museum, Oxford (see *Dalmatian Gems*, p.2ff. and pp.xii–xiii here).

*Foster, Messrs.* see *Odescalchi*

*Glendining & Co.* see *Tripoli*

*Green, William:*
   see **34–6**, **39**, **42**, **84–6**, **103**(?)
The entry for these gems in Montague's catalogue, p.56, reads: 'Nos.565–573 were purchased from Mr Joseph J. Green of Hastings for £3. 10s, May, 1919. They formerly belonged to

William Green, an antiquary of High Wycombe, who died in 1842. Mr J.J. Green states that they have been examined and described by Major Cyril Davenport [typed 'Daunfort'], an authority on gems. I took them to the British Museum, where they were all pronounced genuine excepting nos.565 and 572, which, although not condemned, raised some doubts as to their antiquity.'

*Lawrence, G.F.:*
  see **62–5**
Montague bought a number of antiquities including the lead sealings (ex Nugent coll. – see below) from G.F. Lawrence (or 'Lawrence'). 'Lawrence' also appears as a purchaser of gems in the Odescalchi sale (see below).

*Moore, Major Edward St.Francis* (1853–1940):
  see **24**, **73–4**, **76–7**
Major Moore of 6 Cumberland Street, Woodbridge, Suffolk, supplied a number of gems and other antiquities to Montague. Like Montague he was in the militia and did not serve abroad. He joined the Northamptonshire Regiment in 1877 but retired from it in 1893 (see Hart's *Army List*, 1894). He appears to have been a keen amateur archaeologist and reports of finds made by him at Sutton are recorded in the *Proc. Soc. of Antiquaries*, 2nd s., 10 (1883–5) p.107; and in 11 (1885–7) pp.12–14, 98–9, & 175 he reported on and exhibited finds from near Northampton and sites in Suffolk – including Felixstowe, Woodbridge and Ipswich. Other finds are recorded in 'Notes from Corresponding Members', *Proc. Suffolk Instit. of Archaeol. & Nat. Hist.* 15, pt.i (1913) pp.85–6 and pt.ii (1914) p.226. He left a number of his antiquities to the Ipswich Museum.

An obituary for him appeared in the *Trans. Suffolk Naturalists' Soc.* 4, pt.iii (1940) p.cxviii. The obituary in the *East Anglian Daily Times*, 28/9/40, confuses him with a Major E.C. Moor, an ornithologist and fossil collector.

*Nugent, Baron:*
  see **62–5**
The lead sealings ex Nugent collection were bought by Montague from G.F. Lawrence (see *Lawrence, G.F.* above and p.78)

*Odescalchi, Prince Hugo Erba:*
  see **31–2**
These two gems were said to have been bought at Messrs. Foster's on 10 July 1907. The auction catalogue is entitled: *A Catalogue of the collection of about 4,000 Antique and Modern Rings of his Serene Highness Prince Hugo Erba Odelscalchi [sic] of Budapest, including a number collected by Benedict Odelscalchi [sic] (Innocent XI), who died in 1688. The Collection includes* . . . There are no detailed descriptions or illustrations of gems or rings and as there are often several items in one lot it is not possible to identify them.

The Erba Odescalchi family are descended from Lucretia, the sister of Pope Innocent XI (Benedetto Odescalchi) who had married a member of the Spanish Erba family. It is therefore quite possible that part of the Erba Odescalchi collection had originally belonged to Innocent XI and had somehow passed to Lucretia. This collection should not be confused with the collection of Dom Livio Odescalchi (son of the Pope's brother Charles) which had once belonged to Christina of Sweden (d.1689) and which was later published as the *Museum Odescalchum sive Thesaurus Antiquarum Gemmarium* . . . 2 vols., Rome, 1751 with plates engraved by P.S. Bartoli.

*Tripoli:*

see **29**, **87–93**

The amulets are described in *Bazaar*, 2/7/19 & 9/7/19: 'The next figures illustrate the contents of a lot bought at a sale held by Messrs. Glendining and Co., on 10th April last, and described in the catalogue as "Ancient Egyptian and Sassanian beads, amulets, and seals of cornelian, haematite, pottery and glass, four strings; glass bangles (5); a lachrymatory; glass ring, and another; and an ancient bronze figure of a goat. Some iridescent." These antiquities were taken to Messrs. Glendining by a Servian who had been wounded in the war, and who gave them to understand that he obtained them in Tripoli. The price at which the lot was knocked down was £2 2s.'

## APPENDIX Ia: NOTES ON THE MATERIALS OF THE CYLINDER SEALS

*Chlorite*. Chlorites (H=2.5) are complex hydrated layer silicates of general formula $(Mg,Al,Fe)_{12}(Si,Al)_8O_{20}OH_{16}$ but widespread substitution of these elements takes place. They are generally dark coloured due to their iron content. They occur in metamorphosed terrains such as those relatively close to Mesopotamia in the Zagros mountains and in Northern Syria.

*Carbonates*. The carbonates include examples of limestone, marble and sparry calcite. Limestones are fine-grained sedimentary rocks of very general distribution. They are usually composed of calcite (H=3), a form of calcium carbonate ($CaCO_3$); they are white when pure but can be variously coloured by impurities. Marble, metamorphosed limestone, has a crystalline nature which renders it tougher and less porous than limestone; it is also generally composed chiefly of calcite. Sparry calcite is formed by the crystallization of calcite in veins and cavities.

*Shell*. Shells have layered microstructures and are commonly composed of aragonite (H=3.5), another form of calcium carbonate. The bodies of seals **9** and **10** have microstructures typical of the large columella of meso- or neogastropods which are found in the Indian Ocean (and the Red Sea). However, the unusual shell body of seal **6** appears to have been cut from a rudestid bivalve, possibly *Sphaerulites* which belongs to the family of *Radiolitidae*. This bivalve was akin to a large and thickly walled oyster; it is an Upper Cretaceous fossil, probably about 80 million years old. Strata of this age occur in Northern Iraq and its environs. **6** was tested by Drs Morris, Taylor and Cooper of the Natural History Museum, London.

*Lapis lazuli*. Lapis lazuli (H=4–5.5) is a rock chiefly composed of the bright blue mineral, lazurite $(Na_6Ca_2Al_6Si_6O_{24}[(SO_4),S, Cl,(OH)]_2$. It may also contain white inclusions of calcite and metallic yellowish inclusions of iron pyrites as well as various silicates. It occurs in contact metamorphosed limestones and the lapis lazuli available in Antiquity is thought to have been mined in the Badakshan district of Afghanistan. Its use in Mesopotamia (**4**) was largely restricted to the third millennium BC (G. Herrmann, 'Lapis lazuli: the early phases of its trade', *Iraq* 30,i (1968)).

*Serpentinite*. The serpentine minerals (H=4–6) are complex hydrated layer magnesium silicates of general formula $Mg_3(Si_2O_5)OH_4$ but some substitution, particularly by iron and aluminium takes place. The rock, serpentinite, is often similar in appearance to chlorite; it occurs separately but in similar terrain to chlorite.

*Haematite*. Specular haematite (H=5–6), an iron oxide ($Fe_2O_3$), has a metallic to sub-metallic lustre.

*Quartz*. Quartz (H=6.5–7), the most common of the silica ($SiO_2$) minerals, occurs widely in nature. Chalcedony is a translucent variety of microquartz (fine-grained quartz) which is generally light coloured and without gross colour banding. Carnelian (or cornelian) is a translucent variety of microquartz coloured in shades of red to orange.

*Faience*. Faience, sometimes referred to as composition, sintered quartz or Egyptian faience, was produced by firing quartz sand or ground quartz together with a small proportion of alkali to act as a flux and often, also with a colorant; the surface of the body was usually glazed.

**M. Sax**

## APPENDIX Ib: NOTES ON THE MATERIALS OF THE GREEK, ROMAN AND LATER ENGRAVED GEMS AND AMULETS

*Quartz* ($SiO_2$ – see Appendix Ia). Besides chalcedony and cornelian, a number of other varieties of quartz are represented here: banded agate, layered agate (onyx or sardonyx), heliotrope, jasper (all microcrystalline quartzes) and rock crystal (a macrocrystalline quartz).

*Garnet (var. almandine).* There are a number of varieties of garnet (H=7–7.5). The almandine variety of garnet ($Fe_3Al_2Si_3O_{12}$) was often used for gemstones. The word almandine is said to be derived from Alabanda, a town in west Turkey, where according to Pliny the best stones were cut. Garnet was especially popular in Egypt during the Middle Kingdom when larger specimens were being mined in western Sinai (**87**). There are also references to sources of garnets within the Sassanian empire and so some Sassanian stones were perhaps of native origin (**79**).

*Obsidian.* Obsidian (H=5) is a naturally occurring volcanic glass (often black) which breaks with a concoidal fracture and can be fashioned to a sharp cutting edge. Obsidian comes from various sites in the Middle East, North Africa and the Mediterranean and, although it does not appear to occur in Egypt, it was used there for tools and other objects from predynastic times. It was occasionally used for seals from the archaic period (6th to early 5th century BC) onwards (**54**).

*Talc.* The mineral, talc ($Mg_3Si_4O_{10}(OH)_2$) is very soft (H=1), has a soapy feel and is often greenish white to dark green. Talc is the major constituent of rocks known as steatite or soapstone (**94**).

## APPENDIX 2: EDITION OF THE CUNEIFORM TEXTS WITH NOTES

### (I) GUDEA CONE **PL.G**:
(Corkill, M.15)

| | |
|---|---|
| ᵈnin-gír-su | For (the god) Ningirsu |
| ur-sag kala-ga | the mighty champion |
| ᵈen-líl-lá-ra | of (the god) Enlil, |
| gù-dé-a | Gudea |
| ensí | governor |
| lagašaᵏⁱ-ke₄ | of Lagash |
| nì-du₇-e pa mu-na-è | has performed the proper rites |
| é-ninnu ᵈim-dugudᵐᵘšᵉⁿ-babbár-ra-ni | and (the temple) Eninnu, the shining Im-dugud-bird, |
| | |
| mu-na-dù | he has rebuilt |
| ki-bé mu-na-gi₄ | (and) restored. |
| | |
| | (From Lagash province?) |

## (II) TABLET **PL.H**
(Corkill, T.7)

| | |
|---|---|
| 1 gu₄ še sig₅ | One best barley-fed ox, |
| 2 udu še | two barley-fed sheep, |
| 2 udu 2 silá | two sheep, two lambs, |
| ᵈšara | (for) Shara; |
| 1 gu₄ še sig₅ | One best barley-fed ox, |
| 2 udu še 2 udu | two barley-fed sheep, two sheep, |
| 2 silá | two lambs, |
| ᵈgu-la | (for) Gula; |
| sizkur-sizkur lugala | offerings (on behalf of) the king |
| ki-a-kal-la-ensi | from Akalla, governor |
| umma^ki | of Umma; |
| kišib ᵈnin-MAR.KI-<ka> | sealed by Nin-MAR.KI-ka |
| qa-šu-du₈ | the "libator". |
| itu še-gur₁₀-ku₅ mu-ús-sa | Month of the barley harvest, year after |
| si-ma-num^ki ba-hul | (the year in which) Simanum was destroyed |

The month is the first month of the year in the calendar of Ur; the year-name is that for the 4th year of Shu-Suen = 2034 BC.

Seal impression:

| | |
|---|---|
| ᵈšu-ᵈsuen | Shu-Suen |
| lugal-kala-ga | mighty king |
| lugal urí^ki-ma | king of Ur |
| lugal an-uba-da limmú-ba | king of the four quarters (of the world); |
| ᵈnin-MAR.KI-ka | Nin-MAR.KI-ka |
| qa-šu-du₈ ìr-zu | the "libator" (is) his servant. |

(Possibly from Umma)

## (III) LIMESTONE CYLINDRICAL OR CONOID FRAGMENT (BROKEN AT BOTH ENDS)
(Corkill, M.1)

| | |
|---|---|
| [ᵈba-]-ú | To (the goddess) Bau |
| [mí ša₆]-ga | the good lady |
| [dumu an]-na | daughter of (the god An) |
| [nin-a]-ni | his lady, |
| [gù-d]é-a | Gudea |
| [en]si | governor |
| [lagaš]a    (i.e. [. . . l]a) | of Lagash |
| [^ki-k]e₄ | |
| [a-mu-na]-ru | has presented (this) |

Compare Thureau-Dangin's Statue H, on the basis of which this is restored.

(From Lagash province?)

## (IV) TABLETS
(Corkill, T.1–4)

T.1      Month itu ezen-ᵈme-k[i-gál], 12th month in the calendar of Ur
T.2      Old Babylonian (say 1800 BC), not Ur III, on the basis of the Akkadian personal names.
T.3      Month [itu šeš]-da-kú, 3rd month in the calendar of Ur
T.4      Month itu ezen-ᵈnin-a-zu, 6th month in the calendar of Ur
       (T.5–6 were presented to the British Museum)

(Possibly from Ur)

**Dr C. Walker**


## NOT LOCATED:

Corkill, M.20 – Inscribed brick of Gudea, governor of Lagash, ca.2400 BC. Found at Tello (Girsu) in 1927.
Translated by C.J. Gadd:
'For Ningirsu, the strong warrior of Enlil: Gudea, governor of Lagash, has performed all that is seemly, [and] E-ninnu, of the bright storm-bird, has built for him and restored his place.'
This text appears to be the same as the one on the cone, M.15 (**pl.g**).

# CONCORDANCES

(NL = not located)

## MONTAGUE

| RAM Museum, Exeter acc.no.5/1946 | Montague Cat.no. | Cat.no. |
|---|---|---|
| 352 | 215 | **98** |
| 353 | 353 | **69** |
| 354 | 217 | **29** |
| 355 | 218 | **54** |
| 356 | 219 | **53** |
| 357 | 220 | **81** |
| 358 | 221 | **41** |
| 359 | 222 | (NL) |
| 360 | 223 | **30** |
| 361 | 224 | **97** |
| 362 | 225 | (NL) |
| 363 | 226 | **28** |
| 364 | 227 | **89** |
| 365 | 228 | **90** |
| 366 | 229 | **88** |
| 367 | 230 | **92** |
| 368 | 231 | **"** |
| 369 | 232 | **93** |
| 370 | 233 | **91** |
| 371 | 234 | **94** |
| 372 | 235 | **87** |
| 373 | 236 | **96** |
| 374 | 236a | **83** |
| 375 | 236b | **68** |
| 376 | 236c | **78** |
| 377 | 236d | **67** |
| 378 | 236e | **80** |
| 379 | 236f | **27** |
| 380 | 236g | **72** |
| 381 | 237 | **95** |
| 382 | 238 | **99** |
| 383 | 239 | **32** |
| 384 | 240 | **38** |
| 385 | 241 | **37** |
| 386 | 242 | **40** |
| 387 | 244 | **33** |
| 388 | 243 | **45** |

| RAM Museum, Exeter acc.no.5/1946 | Montague Cat.no. | Cat.no. |
|---|---|---|
| 389 | 245 | 52 |
| 390 | 246 | 48 |
| 391 | 247 | 43 |
| 392 | 248 | 47 |
| 393 | 249 | 49 |
| 394 | 250 | 46 |
| 395 | 251 | (Moved) |
| 396 | 252 | 31 |
| 397 | 253 | (Moved) |
| 398 | 254 | (Moved) |
| 399 | 255 | 50 |
| 400 | 256 | (Moved) |
| 401 | 257 | 82 |
| 402 | 258 | (Moved) |
| 403 | 259 | 51 |
| 407 | 263 | 8 |
| 408 | 264 | 20 |
| 409 | 265 | 19 |
| 410 | 266 | 25 |
| 411 | 267 | 21 |
| 412 | 267a | 24 |
| 436 | 292 | 44 |
| 602 | 469 | 102 |
| 710 | 565 | 85 |
| 711 | 566 | 39 |
| 712 | 567 | 36 |
| 713 | 568 | 42 |
| 714 | 569 | 34 |
| 715 | 570 | 35 |
| 716 | 571 | 86 |
| 717 | 572 | 84 |
| 718 | 573 | 103 |
| 719 | 574 | 74 |
| 720 | 575 | 76 |
| 721 | 576 | 77 |
| 722 | 577 | 73 |
| 758 | 636 | 62 |
| 759 | 637 | (NL) |
| 760 | 638 | 63 |
| 761 | 639 | 64 |
| 762 | 640 | 65 |

## CORKILL

| RAM Museum, Exeter<br>acc.no.86/1966:<br>Corkill no. | Cat.no. |
|---|---|
| S.1 | **6** |
| S.2 | **10** |
| S.3 | **9** |
| S.4 | **13** |
| S.5 | (NL) |
| S.6 | **5** |
| S.7 | **16** |
| S.8 | **7** |
| S.9 | **2** |
| S.10 | **26** |
| S.11 | **23** |
| S.12 | **12** |
| S.13 | **3** |
| S.14 | **14** |
| S.15 | **4** |
| S.16 | **18** |
| S.17 | **15** |
| S.18 | **22** |
| S.19 | **1** |
| S.20 | **17** |
| | |
| M.3 | **101** |
| M.7 | **70** |
| M.8 | **79** |
| M.9 | **66** |
| M.10 | **75** |
| M.12 | **71** |
| M.13 | **100** |

## LOCAL FINDS

| RAM Museum, Exeter no.: | Cat.no. |
|---|---|
| Ant.1278 | **57** |
| 852/1989.1 | **56** |
| 852/1989.2 | **60** |
| 852/1989.3 | **61** |
| 274/1990.G16 | **58** |
| 30/1993.SA1 | **55** |
| 30/1993.SA2 | **59** |

## OTHER

| | |
|---|---|
| 27/1933 | **11** |

MONTAGUE OBJECTS MOVED FROM EXETER TO APPROPRIATE LOCAL MUSEUMS:

5/1946.395 (Mont., no.251)
  Romano-British bronze ring with glass intaglio. (From Ipswich.)

5/1946.397 (Mont., no.253)
  Bronze ring with Greek letter pi Π (?), 𝕁. (From London.)

5/1946.398 (Mont., no.254)
  Iron ring with inscrip. MAVP/IANOV/VIϢI(?) ( = *RIB* 2, fasc.3, p.31, 2422.76.) (In Museum of London.)

5/1946.400 (Mont., no.256)
  Bronze ring with intaglio showing a winged female holding a bunch of grapes. (From Winchester.)

5/1946.402 (Mont., no.258)
  Romano-British(?) bronze ring with face of Jupiter cast in relief. (Found at Hango Hill, nr. Castle Town, Isle of Man.)


MONTAGUE OBJECTS NOT LOCATED:

5/1946.359 (Mont., no.222)
  Gold amulet; eye in centre and apotropaic animals round.

5/1946.362 (Mont., no.225)
  Indian intaglio (cow and calf) mounted in modern silver ring.

5/1946.759 (Mont., no.637)
  Lead sealing (=*RIB* 2, fasc.1, p.95, 2411.42).


CORKILL OBJECTS NOT LOCATED:

S.5 – cylinder seal.

M.11 – described by C.J. Gadd as 'Arab seal inscribed (in reverse) with the name "Muhammad" [i.e. the Prophet]'.

M.20 – Inscribed brick of Gudea, governor of Lagash, ca.2400 BC. Found at Tello (Girsu) in 1927. (See translation at end of Appendix 2.)

# INDEX OF MATERIALS

(Numbers refer to catalogue numbers, not to pages)

Agate:
   banded: **77**
   layered: **49** (etched), **52**, **58** (nicolo glass), **83**, **86** (layered glass), **97** ('eyed'), **102**
   mottled: **100**
Almandine: see Garnet
Bloodstone: see Heliotrope, Jasper
Brass: **82**
Bronze: **28**, **50**, **88–9**, **92**, **98**
Calcite: **7**
Chalcedony: **24–7**, **29**, **67–9**, **78**, **80**, **97**, **102**
Chlorite: **11–16**
Cornelian: **23**, **32**, **34–5**, **37**, **39–40**, **45–6**, **49** (etched), **55–6**, **66**, **72**, **74–6**, **85**, **95** (etched),
    **100** (mottled), **103** (etched)
Faience: **22**, **90–1**
Fossil shell: **6**
Garnet (var. almandine): **79**, **87**
Glass: **30**, **33**, **41**, **44**, **58** (nicolo), **60–1**, **86** (3-layered), **93**, **99**
Granite (micro-): **101**
Haematite: **18**, **20–1**
Heliotrope (jasper): **57**, **59**, **81**, **84**
Iron: **31**, **51** (silvered iron), **71**
Jasper:
   green: **48**, **53**, **73**
   green/red mottled (heliotrope): **57**, **59**, **81**, **84**
   green/white mottled: **47**
   red: **38**, **42–3**
Lapis lazuli: **4**
Lead: **62–5**, **96**
Limestone: **2**, **5**
Marble: **1**, **3**, **17**
Micro-granite (or micro-syenite): **101**
Nicolo (glass): **58**
Obsidian: **54**
Onyx: see Agate, layered
Rock crystal: **36**, **70**
Sardonyx: see Agate, layered
Serpentinite: **8**, **19**
Shell: **6** (fossil), **9–10**
Silvered iron: **51**
Syenite (micro-): **101**
Talc(?): **94**
Turquoise (glass): **33**

# INDEX OF PROVENANCES

(Numbers refer to catalogue numbers, not to pages)

Britain:
  Brough-under-Stainmore (Cumbria): **62–5**
  Dorchester (Durnovaria, Dorset): **50**
  Exeter (Devon): **56–7**, **60–1**
  Seaton Roman villa (Devon): **58**
  Tiverton (Devon): **55**, **59**
Dalmatia:
  Burnum: **37**
  Epidaurum: **38**
  Istria(?): **45**
  Scardona: **40**
Egypt:
  Alexandria: **41**, **51**, **53–4**(?), **81**(?)
Greece:
  Athens?: **97**
Iraq:
  Euphrates river: **69**
  Nineveh: **20**, **25**
  Tello(?) (Girsu): **1–7**, **9–10**, **12–18**, **22–3**, **26**, **66**, **70–1**, **75**, **79**, **100–1**
Palestine:
  Nazareth (Galilee): **52**
  Palestine: **95**
Syracuse(?): see p.78
Syria:
  Tripoli: **29**, **87–93**

# INDEX OF SUBJECTS

(Numbers refer to catalogue numbers, not to pages)

Altar: **48–9**, **80** (fire-holder), **83** (?), **92**
Amphora: **88**
*Ankh* sign: **51**
Antelope: **3**(?), **26**(?), **77**
Anubis (as jackal): **54**
Apollo: **55**
Ares/Mars, bust: **85**(?)
Ariadne: **40**(?)
Athena/Minerva: **36**
Athena/Roma (bust): **85**(?)
Attendant: **10**
Bacchic figures: **40**
Bacchus/Dionysos: **40**(?)
Ball-and-staff: **17**
Bead: **95** (etched cornelian), **100**
Bee: **96**(?)
Bell-clapper: **93**(?)
Bes, Pantheistic: **53**
Bird: **13** (geese), **16** (flying bird(?) & goose), **48** (raven), **49** (eagle), **78**

Bull: **8**, **10**, **24** (human-headed), **73** (zebu)
Bull-man: **8**, **11**(?), **24**
Bust (male): **31–2**, **43**, **66–7**, **68** (king), **84** (emperor?), **85** (Mars/Ares?)
Bust (female): **42**, **85** (Athena/Roma?)
Busts (male and female): **44** (imperial?)
Cactus: **24**
Coin weight: **99**
Combination: **28** (animal/human?), **47** (gryllos), **51** (symbols)
Contest scene: **6–8**, **11–12**, **24–5**
Crescent: see Moon
Cricket: **30**
Crook: **8**(?), **20**
Cross: **98**
Cupid: see Eros/Cupid
Date palm: **14**
Deities (unidentified): see God(s), Goddess(es)
Demeter ( Janiform head): **54**(?)
Device (nišan): **81**
*Dextrarum iunctio*: **49**
Dionysos/Bacchus: **40**(?)
Dioscuri (janiform head): **54**(?)
Dog: **41**(?)
Dolphin: **48**
Eagle: **49**
Emblems: see Symbols
Eros/Cupid: **38–9**, **65**(?)
Eye/face amulet: **97**
Figure(s): **22** (walking in procession), **29** (one standing, one dancing), **60–1** (simplified standing)
Filling motifs: **1**, **3**, **5**, **7–8**, **10–12**, **14–17**, **20**, **23–4**
Fire-holder: **80**
Fish: **2**, **16**(?), **46**
'Gayomard': **69**
Gazelle: **24**, **26**, **77**
Genie (winged): **24–5**
Giant: **86**
Goat: **1**(?), **5**(?), **22**(?), **28**(?), **76**
God(s): **6**, **9**(?), **32** (bust of ?Zeus), **35** (bust)
Goddess(es): **9** (or god?), **10**(?), **13–20**
Goose: **13**, **16**(?)
Grasshopper: **30**
Gryllos: **47**
Hand(s): **49** (clasped), **89–91**
Head(s): **54** (janiform), **82** (masks?) (see also: Bust(s))
Herakles/Hercules: **30**
Hermanubis: **41**
Hermes/Mercury: **37**, **56–7**
Hero: **6–8**, **11–12**, **23**
Horns: **8**(?)
Horse: **59**, **72** (winged), **83**
Horseman: **26**
Human-headed bull: **24** (see also: Bull-man)
Hut (conical reed): **1**
Ibex: **76**

Inscriptions: see **INSCRIPTIONS** below
Insect: **30**, **96**
Intercession scene: see Presentation scene
Isis: **42**(?), **54**(?)
Jackal: **41**, **54**
Janiform head (beardless): **54**
Janus: **54**(?)
Jupiter/Zeus-Serapis: **33** (facing head), **34** (bust)
Kausia: **31**
King: **17** (deified), **18**, **19**(?), **68** (bust)
Knife: **8**
'Legionary' ring: **50**
Libation vessel: **16**
Lightning fork (triple): **20**
Lion: **5–8**, **11–12**, **70–1**
Lion-headed mace (double): **20**
Lion-scimitar: **17**
Lizard: **8**, **16**
Locust: **30**
Mace: **12** (standard), **18**
'Mano fica': **89**(?), **90–1**
Mars/Ares (bust): **85**(?)
Masks(?): **82** (profile facing)
Medusa mask: **52**
Mercury: see Hermes/Mercury
Military standards: **49**
Minerva (Athena): **36**
Monkey: **17**
Monster (quadruped/human): **28**(?)
Moon (crescent): **5**, **7**, **10–11**, **14–17**, **24**
Moon and star disc: **20**
Neptune: **35**(?)
Nergal (monkey, symbol of): **17**
Nišan: **81**
Orion (constellation): **69**
Owl head: **97**(?)
Pantheistic Bes: **53**
Panther: **40**
Pattern (zig-zag): **4**
Pegasus: **45**, **72**
Pendant: **93** (phallic?)
Persephone(?) (janiform head): **54**
Phallus: **91**, **94**
Plant: **1**(?), **3**(?), **9**, **11**(?), **24**, **27**(?), **79** (see also: Tree)
Plough: **9**(?)
Pomegranate plant: **79**
Portrait: see Bust
Poseidon/Neptune: **35**(?)
Pot: see Vessel
Presentation scene: **14–17**
Procession: **22**
Quadruped(s): **1** (horned), **3**, **5–7**, **20**, **22–3**, **26**, **28** (?monster); (see also under names of animals:
    Antelope, Bull, Gazelle, Ibex, Zebu etc.)

Ram: **28**(?)
Raven: **48**
Rosette(s): **5**
*Sa* sign: **51**
Satyr: **58**
Scarab: **87**
Scimitar (lion): **17**
Scorpion: **5**, **16**, **96**
Sealings (lead): **62–5**
Serapis: **33** (facing head), **34** (bust)
Serpent (with janiform head): **54**
Sheep: **5**(?)
Shrine: **1**
Sickle sword: **24**
Sphinx: **25**
Spindle whorl: **101**(?)
Stag: **74–5**
Stamp (Islamic glass): **99**
Standard: **24**, **27** (cross-shaped)
Standard mace: **12**
Star: **3**, **10**(?), **23–4**
Star-disc and crescent: **20**
Stones (cornelian and chalcedony, not engraved): **102–3**
Sun: **5**(?), **10**(?)
Symbols: **27** (divine), **48–9**, **51** (see also: Filling motifs)
Temple: **1**
Thunderbolt: **51**
'Tooth': **92**
Tree: **3**(?), **5**, **10**, **14** (date palm), **15**
Vegetation god or goddess: **9**
Vessel: **1**(?), **16–17**
Wasp: **96**(?)
Weight (Islamic glass): **99**
Winged 'gate': **10**
Winged genie: **24–5**
Worshipper: **9**, **13–17**, **27**
Zebu: **73**
Zeus: **35**(?)
Zeus-Serapis: **33** (facing head), **34** (bust)

## INDEX OF INSCRIPTIONS

(Numbers refer to catalogue numbers, not to pages)

Arabic: **99–100**
Bactrian: **83**
Cufic: **73**
Cuneiform: **11**(?), **12**, **16** (erased), **18–20**
Greek: **54**
Magic: **54**
Pahlavi: **68**
Roman: **50**, **62–4**
Unknown(?): **101** (Archaic Chinese, Indus script?)